BASEBALL AT WAR

WORLD WAR II AND THE FALL OF THE COLOR LINE

THOMAS GILBERT

THE AMERICAN GAME

FRANKLIN WATTS
A Division of Grolier Publishing
New York / London / Hong Kong / Sydney
Danbury, Connecticut

Photographs ©: Transcendental Graphics: 99, 103, 129;
UPI/Corbis-Bettmann: cover, 8, 15, 23, 28, 38, 49, 52, 59, 63, 69,
73, 88, 91, 114, 119.

Library of Congress Cataloging-in-Publication Data

Gilbert, Thomas W.
Baseball at war: World War II and the fall of the color line /
by Thomas Gilbert.
p.   cm. — (The American game)
Includes bibliographical references (p.) and index.
Summary: Discusses the highlights in the game of professional
baseball during the 1940s, including Joe DiMaggio's hitting streak,
the series between the Yankees and the Dodgers, the effects of
World War II on the game, and career of Jackie Robinson.
ISBN 0-531-11330-2
1. Baseball—United States—History—20th century—Juvenile
literature.   2. Afro-American baseball players—History—
20th century—Juvenile literature.   3. World War, 1939–1945—
Juvenile literature.   [1. Baseball—History.]   I. Title.
II. Series: Gilbert, Thomas W. American game.
GV867.5.G55   1997
796.357'0973'09044—dc20   96-34941
                                                                CIP
                                                                 AC

$\mathscr{C}$ONTENTS

The Streak: Joe DiMaggio and 1941

It is curiously difficult to appreciate Joe DiMaggio from statistics alone. His lifetime numbers—.325 BA, 361 home runs, and 1,537 RBIs over 13 seasons—are very good, but they do not seem to justify the reverence in which DiMaggio is held by the generation of fans who saw him play. Part of the reason for this is the fact that he played in Yankee Stadium, a pitcher's park that is murder on right-handed hitters; and Joe DiMaggio's moderate pull-hitting style was particularly unsuited to the Stadium's cavernous left-field power alley. Playing in a neutral park, DiMaggio would have put up numbers a lot more like Lou Gehrig's or Mickey Mantle's; in fact, for their careers on the road DiMaggio outhit the great Ted Williams, .333 to .328.

There is also another reason. DiMaggio was one of those rare players who transcended mere numbers; it was not just what he did, but when he did it, how, and against whom. He was the opposite of the type of player who bats .330 or hits 30 homers without, somehow, seeming to have helped his team win an important game or a big series. Those who lived through DiMaggio's days with the New York Yankees from 1936 to 1951 know that they were watching a player with a special kind of aura about him, an aura that has not only outlasted his playing career but has grown greater over the years as his few faults and imperfections have faded from memory. It inspired the famous line in Simon and Garfunkel's song "Mrs. Robinson"—"Where have you gone, Joe DiMaggio? / A nation turns its lonely eyes to you"—and lends more than a touch of magic to the DiMaggio name even today. To appreciate Joe DiMaggio, you had to be there—and you have to remember.

The DiMaggio legend really began in 1941. He had already played five seasons in the American League, during which time he had won each of the three elements of the Triple Crown at least once; in 1939 and 1940 he won back-to-back batting championships by hitting .381 and .352. But DiMaggio had done little to escape the vast shadows cast by former Yankee greats Babe Ruth and Lou Gehrig. The team had won ten pennants in the heyday of Ruth and Gehrig, but only one since DiMaggio took over as the team's biggest star. DiMaggio had missed about 10 percent of the team's games because of minor injuries or, worse, because of spring training salary holdouts. He was frequently booed by a sizable minority of the Yankee Stadium regulars. The 1940 Yankees of DiMaggio, Joe Gordon, Frank Crosetti, Babe Dahlgren, Red Rolfe, Charlie Keller, George Selkirk, Bill Dickey, Red Ruffing, Marius Russo, and Ernie Bonham came in a very un-Yankee-like third, trailing both the Cleveland Indians, who were led by the young phenom pitcher Bob Feller, and Hank Greenberg's heavy-hitting Detroit Tigers.

THE YEAR: 1940

Already a major-league veteran at 21, Bob Feller had won almost every pitching honor imaginable. He had two AL strikeout titles and had led the league in innings pitched. In 1939, he went 24–9 to lead the AL in wins and complete games. By 1940, just about the only thing Feller had not done was to throw a no-hit game. An overpowering fastball pitcher with a big, hard curve, Feller often took the mound with what ballplayers call "no-hit stuff." Three times, once in 1938 and twice in 1939, he had narrowly missed performing the feat, settling each time for one-hitters; as the 1940 season opened, it seemed only a matter of time before Bob Feller got his no-hitter. Pitching against the Chicago White Sox on Opening Day, Feller put an early end to the suspense and blanked the opposition, 1-0, on no hits. It was the first Opening Day no-no in AL history and the first in the majors since New York Giants pitcher Red Ames lost his Opening Day game in 1909 after pitching ten no-hit frames.

The 1940 season ended much less gloriously than it began for Bob Feller. He lost the pennant-clincher to Detroit on the next-to-last day of the season despite allowing only three hits and two runs. Cleveland finished up with an 89–65 record, one game behind the 90–64 Tigers. Feller had nothing to be ashamed of; the Indians would not have come even that close to a pennant without his 27–11, 2.61 ERA effort. He led the league that season in wins, games, complete games, strikeouts, and innings pitched. Cleveland's weak offense was led by Rookie-of-the-Year shortstop Lou Boudreau, who hit .295 and drove in 101 runs, and first baseman Hal Trosky, who led the team in home runs with 25. Team morale was undermined by an unsuccessful player rebellion against manager Ossie Vitt in the closing days of the race, which culminated with the players presenting a unanimous petition to management demanding Vitt's firing.

In Detroit, new manager Del Baker made the managerial move of the year by putting first baseman Hank Greenberg in left field in order to open up first for a young,

Bob Feller, pictured here at spring training, started the 1940 season with an Opening Day no-hitter. He led the AL that year in wins, games, complete games, strikeouts, and innings pitched.

hard-handed slugger named Rudy York. Greenberg responded with an MVP season: a .340 batting average, a league-high 150 RBIs, 50 doubles, and a league-leading 41 homers. A DH before his time, York contributed 134 RBIs and 33 home runs, and the Tigers as a whole scored a league-leading 888 runs. Charlie Gehringer and Barney McCoskey each batted over .300 to give the Tigers four men with over 100 runs scored. Detroit's pitching staff featured 21–5 Bobo Newsom, third in the league in ERA at 2.83; the 16–3 Schoolboy Rowe; and the 12–9 Tommy Bridges. Both Detroit and Cleveland were momentarily distracted from their mano a mano battle down the stretch by a dramatic late surge from the New York Yankees, who rose from dead last in May to make it a three-team race by season's end. Joe DiMaggio won the batting title, hit 31 homers, and drove in 133 runs.

The Cincinnati Reds took the NL pennant by 12 games over Brooklyn, but the NL race was far from a cakewalk. After starting catcher Ernie Lombardi was knocked out of the line-up by an injury in August, inexperienced back-up catcher Willard Hershberger became overwhelmed by the pressure of playing in a pennant race and committed suicide. A month later, Lombardi reinjured himself seriously, and Cincinnati's 40-year-old coach Jimmy Wilson, who hadn't caught regularly for five years, was activated to take his place. Miraculously, Wilson shook off the rust and skillfully guided the Reds pitchers into the World Series. First baseman Frank McCormick was the team's big gun on offense; he won the NL MVP award on the strength of a league-leading 191 hits, 44 doubles, and 127 RBIs. Cincinnati relied heavily on the pitching duo of Bucky Walters and Paul Derringer, who won 42 games between them. Walters and Derringer led the NL in wins and innings pitched; Walters took the ERA title at 2.48, and teammate Jim Turner came in fourth in ERA at 2.89. Johnny Mize led the league in homers with 43 and RBIs with 137 for third-place St. Louis, and Pittsburgh's Del Garms won the NL batting title at .355.

The Reds won the World Series 4–3 to give the NL its first victory since 1934, when Detroit was also the loser. Walters and Derringer each won a pair of games, but the surprise series hero was coach-turned-catcher Jimmy Wilson, who performed brilliantly on defense and batted .353. Wilson re-retired for good after the season to take a managing job with the Chicago Cubs.

To a modern fan with all the advantages of hindsight, it seems incredible that the Cleveland Indians were favored to win and the Yankees were picked to finish third in 1941. In mid-May, however, things looked even worse than that for New York; Joe DiMaggio had been out for three weeks with a sprained knee and the mighty New Yorkers were dragging. The Yankees were under .500 and on a five-game losing streak; this followed an eight-game losing string earlier that same month. Meanwhile, the Cleveland Indians under new manager Roger Peckinpaugh started the season 28–12 and were threatening to win the AL flag in a runaway.

The Indians were hitting on all cylinders: their smooth-fielding infield of first baseman Hal Trosky, second baseman Ray Mack, shortstop Lou Boudreau, and third baseman Ken Keltner were all contributing with the bat; outfielder Jeff Heath was putting together a career year (.340 BA, 123 RBIs); and Bob Feller had run up 10 wins before June. Feller was the real key to Cleveland's success. One of the earliest examples of a player who was molded into a major-league star by a determined father, the Iowa-born Feller was signed by Indians scout Cy Slapnicka before he graduated from high school, in violation of baseball rules. When an Iowa minor-league club complained to the commissioner, Landis ruled that Feller was entitled to declare himself a free agent and sell his services to the highest bidder. To the relief of Yankee-haters everywhere, the Fellers declined, saying that they were perfectly happy to stay with Cleveland. (The grateful Indians gave Feller a succession of generous contracts; in 1941 Feller was the highest-paid player in the majors after Hank Greenberg.) One look had convinced Slapnicka that the 17-year-old Feller would be wasted in the minors, and he burst upon the major-league scene in 1936 with a 15-strike-out, 4-1 win over the St. Louis Browns. A year later he set a new record for strikeouts in a game with 18, and in 1938 he led the AL in strikeouts for the first of seven times, with 240.

Feller's blazing fastball had become legendary before he was out of his teens. Many were beginning to call it the fastest of all time; all the corny, old anecdotes told about Smoky Joe Wood and Walter Johnson (for example, the batter refusing a third strike or the umpire saying that a pitch "sounded like a strike") were dusted off and retold about Feller. In a famous filmed stunt, Feller's fastball outraced a motorcycle doing 95 MPH. The next stop on Feller's dizzying upward course was a league-high 24 wins in 1939; he also lead the AL in games, shutouts, innings pitched, strikeouts again, and ERA. Then came the 1940 no-hitter. In 1941 Bob Feller would go on to win 25 games and strike out a league-leading 260.

Then, on May 15, 1941, The Streak began. It started with an innocuous little single by DiMaggio off Edgar Smith of the Chicago White Sox. The next day DiMaggio homered and tripled; as the days and then the weeks passed by, a few reporters and fans began to notice that Joe DiMaggio's hitting streak was approaching historic dimensions. DiMaggio himself likes to say that he was unaware of the streak until much later, but this is hard to believe, mainly because DiMaggio had traveled this road before. He actually had a predilection for streaks, those doomed attempts at perfection that are so anti-thetical to the essence of baseball, a game that, above all, demands acceptance of failure and rewards the playing of the percentages. Most people who know about DiMaggio's major-league record 56-game hitting streak in 1941 don't know that immediately afterward he started right in on another streak of 16 games; even fewer are aware that when he was 18 and playing in the Pacific Coast League, he put together a 61-game streak.

Of course, it was hardly big news when Joe started his streak with that May 15 scratch single off left-hander Edgar Smith. Things got interesting around games 25 or 30, when the newspapers began to dust off old hitting-streak marks. Many remembered that St. Louis Browns star George Sisler had put together a streak of 34 games in 1925 and another of 41 in 1922; the legendary Ty Cobb had hit in 35 straight in 1917 and 40 straight in 1911. If the nineteenth century counted—and baseball authorities would differ on this question—then the all-time major-league record was Wee Willie Keeler's 44-game streak, followed by a 42-game effort turned in by .274 lifetime hitter Bill Dahlen—both, not surprisingly, dating from the run-happy 1890s. At the time, however, few fans or sportswriters had heard of either 19th-century streak. The reason for this was that in those days there were no computerized baseball databases, no definitive record books, and no comprehensive baseball encyclopedias like today's *Macmillan* or *Total Baseball*. Records involving such official statistics as wins, ERA, and batting average were kept by the two leagues, but the best baseball writers could do to research more unusual records was to consult newspaper archives, personal scrapbooks, and collections of box scores and scoresheets kept haphazardly by older reporters or fans. Using these methods, it was almost impossible to say with any certainty what the longest hitting streak was or how many players had had streaks of, say, 30 games. Indeed, today we know that several previous long hitting streaks had been forgotten and remained unknown throughout 1941.

As June 1941 wore on, the familiar twentieth-century marks began to fall like dominoes. DiMaggio equaled

Browns first baseman George McQuinn's 1938 34-game streak on June 21. Pressure was building not only on DiMaggio himself but on official scorers, opposing fielders, and especially pitchers, many of whom wanted badly to end the streak but not to cheat posterity by pitching around him. Boston Red Sox star Ted Williams, who was conducting his own assault on the record books by flirting with the first .400 season since Giants first baseman Bill Terry hit .401 in 1930, the Year of the Hitter, later admitted that DiMaggio's amazing streak turned him into a fan as well. Williams played left field in Fenway Park and was normally positioned only a few strides from the park's high left-field wall, known as the Green Monster, which featured a scoreboard operated by a man named Bill Daley. "[Daley] would give me the word on what was going on around the league," Williams later remembered, "all the scores and everything. When DiMaggio was on his hitting streak, Bill would keep track. He'd call out to me from his window in the scoreboard and say: 'Joe just got a double,' and I'd pass it on to [Joe's brother] Dom DiMaggio in center field. [Throughout my career] I was always conscious of the *other* guy. Usually, the guy was Joe DiMaggio."[1]

As DiMaggio's streak cruised into the thirties, New York fans were momentarily distracted by another streak. The pennant-winning 1940 Detroit Tigers had set an AL team record with 17 straight games with at least one home run. Now the Yankees were mounting a challenge to that record; the Yankees tied Detroit's mark in an unlikely way when little shortstop Phil Rizzuto swatted his second career homer off Tigers pitcher Dizzy Trout. A day later, DiMaggio extended the team homer streak to 18 and his personal hitting streak to 35 with a game-winning home run to right field; the day after that, Rolfe, Henrich, and Gordon all homered, while DiMaggio waited for his final at bat to collect his only hit on the day, a single. The morning newspaper headlines show that the DiMaggio streak had not yet become the most important event of the 1941 season. "YANKS EXTEND HOMER STREAK TO 19 GAMES," blared one New York paper over the subheadline: "DiMaggio Hits in 36th Straight with Single in Last At Bat."

DiMaggio's teammates were the first to notice that something very special was happening. Phil Rizzuto said:

> *He always hit the ball well. Very seldom, if ever, would he hit a ball on the handle or on the end of the bat, like most of us "normal" ball players. Every time he hit it, it was almost always good wood. But now he was outdoing himself. Everything he hit was a bullet. I'll never forget Joe telling me once—and he's the only man that ever said it, the only man who could ever say it—that he could hit a ball with the third baseman playing deep and still handcuff him. In other words, if he hit a low line drive and the third baseman had his hands on his knees, the ball would be by him before he could actually get set to field it.*[2]

On June 26, DiMaggio's teammates helped him extend the streak to 38. In his first three at bats of game 38, DiMaggio had flied out, reached on an error, and grounded out. With Marius Russo sailing through the late innings with a 3-1 victory, it suddenly became apparent that there would be no bottom of the ninth; and with DiMaggio scheduled to bat fourth in the bottom of the eighth, at least one Yankee would have to reach base for DiMaggio to have a chance to keep the streak going. The small Yankee Stadium crowd breathed a sigh of relief when Red Rolfe drew a walk in the eighth inning. The next batter was right fielder Tommy Henrich; then came DiMaggio. But Henrich had a horrible thought as he walked toward the plate: What if he

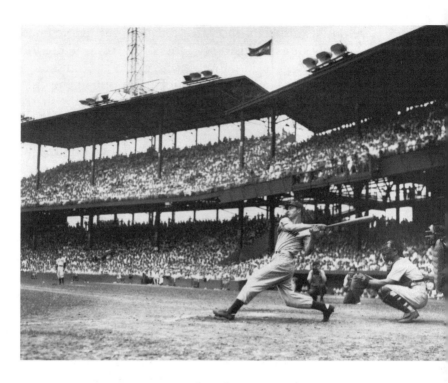

Joe DiMaggio smacks a hit against the Washington Senators on June 29, 1941. DiMaggio's incredible 56-game hitting streak in 1941 started on May 15 and was snapped on July 17.

hit into a double play, costing DiMaggio his last chance to continue the streak? Henrich stopped, turned to manager Joe McCarthy and asked for permission to lay down a bunt, something an RBI man like Henrich was rarely, if ever, called upon to do. McCarthy said yes; and Henrich sacrificed beautifully. Swinging at the first pitch, DiMaggio then followed with a ringing double down the third-base line.

In game number 40, DiMaggio faced Athletics right-hander Johnny Babich, a pitcher who made no bones about his dislike of the New York Yankees. Babich had publicly threatened to stop the streak by walking the Yankees slugger three times if he could get him out in his first at bat. DiMaggio did make out in the first inning; in the fourth, however, he extended his streak by reaching out and poking a single off a 3-0 pitch that Babich had purposefully thrown a foot outside. A week later, when he passed Sisler's AL record of 41—then widely believed to be the all-time major-league record—Joe DiMaggio and The Streak had become national sensations. In a July 2nd game in Boston, after DiMaggio had been dramatically robbed twice by great catches in the outfield—one by his brother Dom—he homered off Red Sox pitcher Dick Newsome in the fifth to tie the major-league record of 44 games set by Wee Willie Keeler back in 1897, before foul balls counted as strikes. He got number 45 off tough knuckleball/spitball pitcher Dutch Leonard to break the all-time record. After the game, an obviously relieved DiMaggio told reporters: "It's all over now and I'm glad of it. Now I can go back to swinging at good pitches again—if I get them. I'm kind of sick of going after anything they throw up there—just so I wouldn't be walked."

But The Streak was not over. It lasted two more weeks, reaching 56 games by the time the Yankees played the Indians before 67,468 screaming Cleveland fans on July 17. As things turned out, it was defense—Cleveland's all–Gold Glove infield—not an opposing pitcher, that finally brought Joe DiMaggio's streak to an end. In his first at bat, DiMaggio drove the ball down the left-field line, where third baseman Ken Keltner dove for it, backhanded. Keltner played eleven seasons with the Cleveland Indians. Although no Hall of Famer, Keltner was the finest fielding third baseman of the 1940s. He regularly led the league at his position in assists, fielding, and double plays, turning 37 in 1944, 38 in 1942, and 40 in 1939. Keltner could hit, too, producing around 30 doubles, 9 triples, and 20 homers in an average season. Twice he drove in over 110 runs, and in 1948 he showed a characteristic ability to rise to the occasion, producing a career year—.297 with 91 runs, 31 homers, and 119 RBIs—that helped propel Cleveland to an AL pennant and a World Series victory. On July 17, 1941, Keltner lunged across the foul line to make a diving stop of DiMaggio's hot grounder, fired to first, and barely nipped DiMaggio, who was slightly slowed by a Cleveland infield still soggy from a recent rain. Pitcher Al Smith walked DiMaggio his second time up, provoking boos from the Indians fans in the stands. In his third at bat, DiMaggio hit a ball to Keltner's right that was a carbon copy of the one he had hit in the first inning. Once again, Keltner backhanded it deftly and threw DiMaggio out. The Streak ended for good in the eighth inning when, facing reliever Jim Bagby Jr. (the son of 1910s and 1920s pitcher Jim Bagby Sr.) with the bases loaded, Joe hit a hard grounder up the middle that appeared to take a sudden bad hop toward the glove of shortstop Lou Boudreau, who flipped the ball to second baseman Ray Mack to start a 6-4-3 double play. After the game, DiMaggio expressed relief but admitted: "I can't say I'm glad it's over. I wanted it to go on as long as it could."

When you look at a statistical summary of The Streak, DiMaggio's feat appears even more miraculous. Overall he batted .408, which is relatively low considering that he had to distribute only 91 hits over the 56 games. He made four hits in a game only four times and kept the streak alive with a single hit a hair-raising 34 times. On several occasions the streak hung by the slenderest of threads—many of them, curiously, coming against the White Sox. In games number 30 and 31, DiMaggio got bad-hop singles off the body of White Sox shortstop Luke Appling, and in number 54 his only hit was an infield dribbler that Chicago third baseman

Bob Kennedy could not make a play on. While he handled Cleveland ace Bob Feller fairly well, going 2-6 for a .333 batting average, DiMaggio's great pitching nemesis was obscure White Sox righty Johnny Rigney, a 63–64 pitcher over eight big-league seasons. DiMaggio faced Rigney four times during the streak and barely managed to squeak by, going 1-3, 1-5, 1-4, and 1-3 for a .267 average. Another peculiarity of The Streak was that it was ended by the son of a former major-league pitcher, just as his PCL streak of 61 games had been ended by Ed Walsh Jr., the son of spitball legend and Hall of Famer Ed Walsh.

Perhaps the oddest thing about Joe DiMaggio's hitting streak is its tremendous mathematical improbability. To put it simply, it makes no sense for even a great hitter to be able to get at least one hit every day for such a long period. Certainly, many great hitters who were in Joe DiMaggio's class have never come close to a 56-game hitting streak. To give an idea of how improbable The Streak really was, one statistician has calculated that a baseball league in which there would be at least a 50 percent chance of one player putting together a 50-game hitting streak in a given season would have to contain 52 lifetime .350 batters (over 1,000 games) and *four* lifetime .400 hitters. In the history of the real major leagues, of course, no one has ever come remotely close to batting .400 for a career, and only three men— Ty Cobb, Rogers Hornsby, and Joe Jackson—have had career batting averages over .350. Adding to the improbability of The Streak is the fact that as it went on, DiMaggio performed under ever-increasing pressure and scrutiny—something that should have hurt his performance. In 1941, however, Joe DiMaggio actually hit better as the streak continued. He batted only .362 in the first 18 games of the streak and .367 over the next dozen games. After game 30, however, when fans began to pay attention to the streak for the first time, he batted .457. DiMaggio then batted an incredible .510 after breaking Wee Willie Keeler's mark of 44, a time when the whole nation was watching and DiMaggio was playing under a distracting barrage of media and public pressure. The 56-game hitting streak has stood unchallenged for more than half a century—the closest a modern hitter has come was Reds star Pete Rose's 44-game streak in 1978—and it has grown into one of the prime components of the DiMaggio legend. Among the long list of immortal baseball feats, The Streak remains particularly inspiring because it runs so contrary to the iron laws of probability that govern the lives of ordinary human beings. DiMaggio's streak was as big a long shot as winning the lottery and, at the same time, so obviously not the result of mere luck. As Stephen Jay Gould has written: "DiMaggio's hitting streak is the finest of legends because it embodies the essence of the battle that truly defines our lives. He cheated death, at least for a while."

CHAPTER TWO

The Kid: Ted Williams and 1941

Ted Williams and Joe DiMaggio missed becoming teammates by $1,000. That was the amount Ted's mother Mrs. Williams demanded from the New York Yankees as the price for allowing her son to sign a contract in 1936. At the time, fellow Californian Joe DiMaggio was causing a sensation as a rookie center fielder for the Yankees and Ted Williams was a tall, skinny kid from San Diego who had hit .586 and .403 in two years of high school ball. The son of a physically absent father and an emotionally absent mother who was known as "Salvation May" for her fanatical devotion to the Salvation Army, Williams's first ambition was to become a fireman. This changed around age 14 when the deceptively strong teenager discovered what he could do with a bat, a baseball, and a pent-up desire to get even with the world. When the Yankees said no to the $1,000 bonus, Williams was snatched up by Eddie Collins of the Boston Red Sox. After a few years of seasoning in the minors, Williams broke into the Boston lineup in 1939 with one of the great rookie performances in baseball history: a .327 batting average, 44 doubles, 11 triples, 31 home runs, and 145 RBIs. He was 20 years old.

A brash egotist with a driving ambition to become, as he plainly admitted, "the greatest hitter who ever lived," Williams practiced strike-zone discipline as though it were a religion; he intimidated pitchers with his burning intensity and his ability to take calmly pitches one inch off the plate while in the same at bat swinging with all-out aggression at a strike. Ted Williams achieved a unique combination of patience and power. He drew 2,019 walks in his 2,292 major-league games, while at the same time swatting 521 homers; second only to Babe Ruth in career slugging average, Williams's career on-base average of .483 remains the highest mark of all time. (Babe Ruth is second in this category at .474.) As Yankee Vic Raschi, a pitcher who was known as an intimidator himself, put it, "What do you do with a guy that's been staring at you from the moment he's left the on-deck circle, and keeps his eyes on your eyes when he steps into the batter's box? Ted's concentration was so intense I don't think he even knew what I was trying to do." In 1941, Ted Williams may well have been the greatest hitter in the game, but he had a rival for the greatest *player*— Joe DiMaggio. If DiMaggio could not quite hit with Williams, he was a far better fielder and base runner and, to many, a far better person and a superior team player. Throughout the 1940s and into the 1950s, Williams and DiMaggio led their teams in a series of epic pennant battles that constitute the glory days of the ancient Yankees–Red Sox rivalry, baseball's oldest and most venerable intercity rivalry. Both saw their careers interrupted by war. Today these two men are forever connected in baseball lore, as identified with their teams and their eras as any two players in baseball's long history. Years after the fact, fans still react with horror when the story is told of the night that the owners of the Yankees and the Red Sox came within a whisker of swapping Williams and DiMaggio for each other, straight up.

Joe DiMaggio and Ted Williams were more than contemporaries and personal rivals; they were two of the greatest stars in baseball history. Baseball greatness, however, comes in many forms. On the field and off, the slow-footed Red Sox slugger and the graceful Yankees center fielder were as different from each other as two players could be. Ted Williams certainly played hard, but his goals seemed somehow more selfish than Joe DiMaggio's. The difference in their philosophies is captured by two famous quotes that more or less sum up both men's careers. "I want to walk down the street after I'm through," Williams once said, "and have people say, 'There goes the greatest hitter who ever lived.'" Asked by an interviewer why he played so hard when he was hurt, DiMaggio answered: "I can't explain it, even to myself. Something inside just kept saying: 'Play ball all the time as hard as you can—and win.'" No season illustrates this better than 1941, when both performed marvels that have been unequaled since, but in very different ways and with very different results. DiMaggio had The Streak, batted .357 for the season, and led the Yankees to the AL pennant. Williams became the last batter to hit over .400, led DiMaggio in on-base average .551 to .440 and in slugging .735 to .643—and the Red Sox finished in the Yankees' dust by a margin of 17 games.

A lifetime .344 hitter who won the triple crown in 1941, 1942, and 1947 (four triple crowns in seven years if you include the minor-league triple crown he won with the Minneapolis Millers of the American Association in 1938), who hit over .320 in 12 of his 13 full seasons, and who won seven batting titles, Ted Williams was a good candidate to bat .400 primarily because of his

Ted Williams displays his batting stance before a July 1941 game. Williams hit .406 that season, the last major-league player to hit .400 or better.

terrific strike-zone judgment. Thanks to his amazing vision—U.S. Navy doctors tested his eyes during World War II and found that Williams's eyesight was equaled by only 6 people out of 10,000—Williams's batting eye may well have been the best of all time. Eleven times he drew over 100 walks in a season and three times he drew over 160. Besides the fact that it put opposing pitchers under pressure to throw strikes, giving him better pitches to hit, Williams's willingness to accept walks meant that in his full seasons he averaged only 490 at bats, and it is certainly a lot easier to bat .400 in 490 at bats than it is in 590.

Of course, it is never easy to hit .400, even in eras that favor offense; after all, there have been only 27 .400 seasons in the 125-year history of major-league baseball. Hugh Duffy—who, coincidentally, served as a coach with the 1941 Red Sox and personally rooted Ted Williams on—recorded the highest single-season batting average ever, .440, but Duffy's achievement, like more than half of all .400 seasons, came in the run-happy days before the foul-strike rule. Implemented in the NL in 1901 and the AL in 1903, the foul-strike rule required that foul balls be counted as strikes until the second strike; before then, foul balls were not counted at any time in the count. The rest of the .400 seasons before 1941 all came between the advent of the cork-centered baseball in 1911 and the peak year of the home-run era, 1930. Since New York Giant Bill Terry had hit .401 that year, no hitter had come closer to the magic .400 mark than Al Simmons's .390 in 1932. In the 55 years since Ted Williams's .400 season in 1941, no one has come closer than Kansas City Royal George Brett's .390 in 1980.

Still, as Williams often admitted, there were several things working in his favor in 1941. One was that the Boston Red Sox happened to play in Fenway Park, a tremendous hitters' park that discourages the home run but greatly increases nearly every other offensive statistic, especially batting average. A good illustration of how much Fenway helped Williams throughout his career is that, though Williams outhit DiMaggio for their careers by 19 points, .344 to .325, DiMaggio actually outhit Williams in neutral road parks by five points, .333 to .328. Another lucky accident for Williams in 1941 was a minor leg injury that limited his season to 456 at bats and spared him two weeks of playing in the bitter cold Boston April weather that he despised. Williams also likes to tell the story of how an obscure pitcher named Joe "Burrhead" Dobson was a big factor in his .400 season. Early on in the season, when Williams's leg was on the mend and Dobson happened to be relegated to spot-starting duty, both players decided to keep in shape by playing simulated games against each other each morning. During these practice sessions Dobson liked to bear down hard, using his whole pitching repertoire, and according to Williams, "[I got] the most batting practice of my life, and the best." When he returned to the regular Boston lineup, Ted Williams did not have to search for his batting stroke.

THE YEAR: 1941

Joe DiMaggio outperformed Ted Williams in the pennant race and in the MVP voting in 1941, but when their paths crossed in the All-Star game, held in Detroit on July 8, it was Williams who stole center stage from his Yankees rival. DiMaggio hit a single—no surprise, with the All-Star game coming smack in the middle of his 56-game hitting streak—but the American League went into the ninth down 5-4, thanks to Pirates shortstop Arky Vaughn, who had launched two-run homers in the seventh and eighth. Batting against Cubs righthander Claude Passeau with two outs, Williams turned on a 2-1 fastball, blasting the pitch into the distant right-field upper deck to win the game for the AL, 7-5. According to one newspaper account, "With an ear-to-ear grin Williams leaped into the air and clapped his hands like a little boy before sheepishly trotting around the bases." Coming at a time when the All-Star game excited much greater fan interest than it does today and when the rivalry between the two major leagues was taken very seriously on and off the field, this was one of the most dramatic and emotional All-Star contests ever.

The New York Yankees won the 1941 pennant by a wide margin over Boston, but the pennant race was dominated by the personal heroics of AL MVP Joe DiMaggio, who put together a record 56-game hitting streak, and Boston's Ted Williams, who batted .406. DiMaggio started his 1941 streak against the White Sox on May 15. On July 2, a DiMaggio homer broke Wee Willie Keeler's 44-year old major-league hitting-streak mark of 44, and on July 17 his streak was ended at 56 by two terrific back-handed stops by Indians third baseman Ken Keltner.

Joe DiMaggio finished the season third in the AL in batting average, first in RBIs with 125, second in doubles with 43, and fourth in home runs. But his season was overshadowed statistically by that of Boston's Ted Williams, who led him in runs (135-122), and homers (37-30), as well as in on-base average and slugging average. Williams batted .406, 47 points higher than Washington's Cecil Travis and 49 points better than DiMaggio. This was the highest batting average in either league since Rogers Hornsby's .424 in 1924. To put Williams's feat in perspective, consider that for the entire season Williams batted only three points lower than DiMaggio did during his amazing 56-game hot streak, (.406 to .408).

A teammate of Williams, Red Sox pitcher Lefty Grove, won his 300th game at the age of 41 and promptly retired with a 300–141 lifetime record. Pitching for the

Philadelphia Athletics and Boston, Grove compiled a lifetime 3.06 ERA pitching exclusively in hitters' parks and in a hitters' era, won an unapproachable nine ERA titles, and led the AL in strikeouts seven times in a row.

In the NL, Brooklyn won a tight race over St. Louis thanks mostly to MVP Dolph Camilli's league-leading 34 homers and 120 RBIs and rookie outfielder Pete Reiser's NL-high .343 batting average, 117 runs, 39 doubles, and 17 home runs. Besides Reiser, who was plucked from Branch Rickey's famous St. Louis farm system, the Dodgers roster was loaded with ex-Cardinals, including Ducky Medwick, manager Leo Durocher, and catcher Mickey Owen. Brooklyn pitchers Whitlow Wyatt and Kirby Higbe led the NL in wins, and Wyatt was second in ERA to the Reds' Elmer Riddle at 2.34.

The first Dodgers-Yankees World Series looked like it was headed for at least six games when, with New York leading two games to one, Brooklyn's ace reliever Hugh Casey took a 4-3 lead into the ninth inning of game four. With two outs and nobody on, Casey struck out Yankees outfielder Tommy Henrich, but Owen could not block the ball and Henrich reached first base. DiMaggio singled, Keller doubled, Dickey walked, and Gordon doubled to steal the game from the Dodgers by a score of 7-4. The next day the Yankees clinched the series on Ernie Bonham's four-hit, 3-1 victory.

Like DiMaggio, Ted Williams in 1941 was a great player just beginning to come into his own as a superstar. After his sparkling rookie year, Williams had hit a gaudy .344 with 43 doubles, 23 home runs, and 113 RBIs in 1940, but few were ready to put him in the same category as Greenberg, Feller, and the other members of the game's elite. The main reason for this was his nettling personality; not only did Williams seem unable to get along with sportswriters and fans, he did not seem to care much, either. In the words of one con-

*In the first game of the 1941 World Series,
Yankees catcher Bill Dickey tags out a sliding
Dodger at the plate. The Yankees won the first
Dodgers-Yankees World Series series 4–1.*

temporary writer, Williams was "headstrong, surly, mer-
curial, petulant, sulking, pouting, insecure, emotionally
undeveloped, and a problem child." He alienated team

leader Jimmie Foxx by loafing down the line on ground-ball outs. Instead of ignoring hecklers, Williams traded insults with them and made himself look foolish. The Fenway fans started booing him. In one unpleasant incident, he actually spat at a fan; on another occasion he threw a typewriter at a reporter whose column made him angry.

Ted Williams tended to blame everyone but himself for his problems, but early on in 1941 it seemed as though he had found a way to take out his frustrations on the baseball. He started the season on fire, batting .333 in the middle of May. His batting average rose steadily through Memorial Day, when a six-hit double-header raised his average to .429. Propelled, ironically enough, by a 23-game hitting streak that began the day before DiMaggio's streak, he reached as high as .436 in early June and stayed above .400 through mid-summer. At the All-Star break he was batting .405, 70 points higher than the streaking DiMaggio. Then came a grad-ual decline that coincided with the arrival of the colder, early autumn weather. Up to .413 in September, he fell to .3995 with a double header remaining to play against Philadelphia on the last day of the season. Because, by contemporary baseball rules, .3995 would round out to an official .400, Red Sox manager Joe Cronin urged him to sit the games out and preserve his record season. But Ted Williams refused to back into a .400 season or win it on a technicality; he insisted on playing. That day everyone from the fans in the stands to plate umpire Bill McGowan to the official scorer was nervous, but nothing could stop Williams, who played both ends of the doubleheader and went 6-8 with a home run to hit .406 the hard way.

As with Joe DiMaggio and The Streak, 1941 was the beginning of the legend of Ted Williams—known to this day as "the last man to bat .400." As Robert Creamer wrote in his book *Baseball in '41,* "Those blazing weeks in the spring and early summer of 1941 were when Williams came of age as a hitter, when he began to be accepted as a great baseball player. Everyone knew by then that he was a lot more than a pouty juvenile who wanted to be a fireman. He was Ted Williams. He was a force."[1]

The AL season of 1941 raises two interesting questions. One, who was the greater player, DiMaggio or Williams? And second, which was the greater achievement, Williams's .406 or DiMaggio's 56-game streak? As for the first, most baseball fans then and now would probably agree with Ted Williams's own assessment that DiMaggio was a better all-around player, but that "I was a better hitter than Joe." On the second point, however, Williams's and DiMaggio's contemporaries were squarely with Joe DiMaggio. How could a 56-game streak of .408 hitting compare to an entire season of hitting .406? Amazingly enough, to the sportswriters who saw the games that year, it was not really even close. Exhibit A is the AL MVP vote for that year, in which the writers gave the award to DiMaggio by a comfortable margin of 291 points to 254 for Williams; Bob Feller finished third with 174 points. Why? Clearly, the answer is the difference in the two players' influence on the AL pennant race. In spite of Ted Williams's amazing hitting, the Boston Red Sox were never much of a factor in the race, spending most of the season hovering around .500 and finishing 17 games out despite putting on a September salary drive that put the team in second place. The Red Sox scored the most runs in the AL and led the league in doubles, team batting, and team slugging average. A breakdown of the Yankees' season, however, shows that DiMaggio's streak was far more than an individual tour de force; during those 56 games DiMaggio put the Yankees on his back and carried them out of their spring doldrums and into first place. Thanks to DiMaggio, the Yankees improved from a 25–22 record on June 6 to 48–26 at the All-Star break. During the six or so weeks that The Streak lasted, DiMaggio hit 16 doubles, 4 triples, and 15 home runs; he scored 56 runs and knocked in 55. He walked 21 times and struck out only 7 times. The bottom line on Ted Williams's record-setting season? Like the rest of the Red Sox that year, Williams in 1941 was all flashy hitting stats and no flag. The bottom line for DiMaggio's 1941 season? On the day that DiMaggio's streak began, the Yankees were in fourth place and slipping; on the day it came to an end, the Yankees completed a 17-wins-out-of-18-games run and led the rest of the AL by seven games. DiMaggio and the Yankees never looked back. The pennant race was over and, as usual, the team that had Joe DiMaggio on it was the winner.

CHAPTER THREE

$\mathscr{B}$alata and Oleomargarine: Baseball Survives the War Years

For the fans who lived through DiMaggio's streak, Williams's successful assault on .400 and the many other great achievements and great moments of that year, 1941 seemed bathed in a kind of magical glow that gave the baseball played that year a special, heightened quality. (Interestingly enough, the cricket seasons that were played just before the outbreak of World War II are remembered in much the same way by English sports fans.) The reason for this may well have been that the 1941 season played out against the backdrop of the gathering world war. Many Americans spent that year trying very hard to pretend that their country was not going to have to join in the fighting. Those who were baseball fans focused a little harder on the sports pages, as if by doing so they might avoid being affected by the dark news from Poland, China, and France that filled the front of the paper.

Momentum for what would become World War II began to build in the early 1930s, as the fascist Adolf Hitler took and then consolidated power in Germany,

32

the Japanese threw their military weight around in the Far East, and the League of Nations—the precursor of today's United Nations, which had been founded in the aftermath of the first world war—fell apart. Giving an ominous hint of its ultimate intentions, Japan shut down its professional baseball leagues in 1941 on the grounds that they represented a corrupting American influence. In 1937, President Franklin Roosevelt signed the Neutrality Act, an attempt to keep the United States from being drawn into the European or Asian conflicts. In 1938, while maintaining a position of strict noninvolvement in any foreign war, Roosevelt authorized a massive building project to expand both the Atlantic and Pacific fleets of the U.S. Navy. That same year saw Germany annex a large part of its neighbor Czechoslovakia; the future Allied powers sold out their Czechoslovak allies and caved in to Hitler, thinking that they were averting war by appeasing him. They were dead wrong. Less than a year later, World War II began in earnest. Encouraged by his enemies' indecisiveness, Hitler seized the remainder of Czechoslovakia and negotiated the German-Russian Non-Aggression Pact, which freed Germany to invade large portions of Eastern Europe without fear of attack from Stalin's mighty Russian military. German tanks rolled into Poland and, a little later, into Finland. In September 1939, Great Britain and France declared war on Germany.

Americans, however, spent much of the years 1940 and 1941 in a state of denial about the inevitability of their country's participation in World War II. In October 1940 the reality of the war first touched the lives of ordinary American men as all those between 21 and 36 were required to register for the Selective Service and some, to their surprise, were immediately drafted. A few of these first draftees were baseball players; Phillies pitcher Hugh Mulcahy became the first active major leaguer to change from flannels into fatigues. As in the previous world war, the first instinct of most Americans was to avoid involvement at all costs; when the time came that their government became committed to going to war, it took a skillful propaganda campaign and a powerful appeal to their patriotism to overcome this instinct. World War I was a case in point. Several months of patriotic noise and phony newspaper stories about Germans raping Belgian nuns and crucifying young Canadian soldiers transformed a public that had stubbornly resisted involvement in the gruesome European bloodbath into flag-waving, enthusiastic war supporters. Convinced that World War I was a "good war" and that democracy and the American way of life were somehow threatened by the presence of German troops in France and Belgium, young men volunteered for military service by the hundreds of thousands.

These periodic outbreaks of war fever in American history have always carried with them a subtle threat. Though it may be acceptable to oppose the war beforehand, once the nation has declared war Americans are expected to close ranks. Those who dissent risk having their patriotism called into question. Sure enough, as soon as the America of 1918 had turned 180 degrees and joined the fighting in World War I, pacifists (people who oppose all war for religious or other moral reasons) and other prominent opponents of the war, like Socialist Congressman Victor Berger of Wisconsin and union activist Bill Haywood, were reviled as traitors, prosecuted, and in some cases even imprisoned. One of the little signs in 1941 of how far American public opinion had swung toward support for World War II is an article from April that appeared in the *Spalding Guide,* the official baseball annual. Entitled "Baseball Never a Slacker," it asserts baseball's patriotism and cites the game's participation in previous wars. Used in the late 1910s for a man who evaded military service, the term "slacker" carried a definite implication of cowardice.

The major leagues were defensive on this point because during World War I they had come off looking selfish by unsuccessfully appealing for a blanket exemption for their players from the government's "work-or-fight" order. In the fall of 1918, while American soldiers were fighting and dying in Europe, baseball staged an embarrassing squabble, including a brief strike, between players and owners over World Series profits. Many players took their military obligations less than seriously; Chicago Cubs pitcher Harry Weaver, for example, asked for a draft deferment on the grounds that "we have a good chance to win the pennant." A continuing source of scandal were the many big-league teams who evaded the order by securing no-show jobs for star players in defense-related factories. Red Sox pitcher Babe Ruth was one of the many able-bodied young ballplayers who was accused of dodging the draft.

Fortunately for baseball, things were different in World War II. After the December 1941 Japanese attack on Pearl Harbor finally provoked the United States to declare war on Germany and Japan, baseball commissioner Kenesaw Mountain Landis wrote a letter to President Roosevelt, a big baseball fan, inquiring about his views on how and whether professional baseball should continue during wartime. The superpatriotic and rabidly anti-German Landis made no plea for special treatment; not only had he been a prominent critic of baseball's behavior during World War I, but Landis was also the federal judge who, before he had any involvement with baseball, had handed down stiff sentences in both the Victor Berger and the Bill Haywood cases. Roosevelt, however, answered Landis with the famous "Green Light" letter. Saying, "I honestly feel that it would be best for the country to keep baseball going; these players are a definite recreational asset to at least 20 million of their fellow citizens," he granted professional baseball a privileged status on the grounds that the game was essential to the national morale. Players with draft deferments would be allowed to continue their careers and those without them would have to go to war; the fans would not be left wondering what strings their team had pulled to keep its cleanup hitter out of the army.

The 1942 season proceeded without any drastic effects from the war. A number of minor leagues folded, including the Texas League, but few major-league stars were drafted. The New York Yankees lost Tommy Henrich, but Joe DiMaggio, Joe Gordon, Phil Rizzuto, Ernie Bonham, Spud Chandler, and most of the rest of the team stayed. The 1942 Yanks repeated as AL champs by nine games over Boston, who still had second baseman Bobby Doerr, shortstop Johnny Pesky, center fielder Dom DiMaggio, pitcher Tex Hughson, and the great Ted Williams. Many big-league stars played the 1942 season in a kind of limbo, not sure what was expected of them. Joe DiMaggio, for example, registered for the draft and was classified 3-A, which meant that he was not in immediate danger of being drafted because he was the sole provider for his wife, actress Dorothy Arnold, and child, Joseph Paul DiMaggio Jr., who had been born in October 1941. In spring training of 1942 he answered questions about why he had not volunteered for military service by saying that he was reserving $5,000 of his yearly salary to buy war bonds. He played out the 1942 season but did not perform particularly well. Whether the reason was the war or his deteriorating marriage (DiMaggio and Arnold separated in late 1942 and divorced in 1944), DiMaggio batted an uncharacteristically mortal .305 with 21 home runs and 114 RBIs.

New York–born Hank Greenberg almost singlehandedly lived down the memory of baseball's poor showing during World War I. One of baseball's rare Jewish stars, Greenberg remained ever-conscious of the casual anti-Semitism of American life in the 1930s and 1940s and of his status as a conspicuous representative of all Jews for many ordinary Americans. He knew well that many people would judge all American Jews by his behavior and he made sure to present a clean-cut, All-American image. Drafted in May 1941—Greenberg played only 19 games that year—he enthusiastically reported to Fort Custer, Michigan and joined an anti-tank unit. "I never asked for a deferment," Greenberg commented, "I made up my mind to go when I was called. My country comes first." A U.S. senator from North Carolina praised Greenberg for willingly giving up a $55,000-a-year job "to serve his country at $21.00 a month." "To my mind," the senator continued, "he's a bigger hero than when he was knocking home runs." Discharged on December 5, 1941, Greenberg reenlisted immediately after the Japanese attack on Pearl Harbor, becoming the first big-league star to volunteer; Indians pitcher Bob Feller joined up a few days later. Greenberg was 30 years old and in his prime; Feller was 24. Between them, they would lose a total of 8½ seasons to World War II.

Red Sox star Ted Williams, already saddled with the burden of his reputation for selfishness, had a much more difficult time of it in 1942. Though single, Williams had originally been classified 3-A as the sole support of his mother. Virtually penniless and abandoned by her husband, Williams's mother was in fact completely dependent on Ted. After Pearl Harbor, however, cases like these were routinely changed to 1-A and few Red Sox fans counted on seeing Williams in a Boston uniform in 1942. Then in February of that year the newspapers carried the surprising news that Williams had received a draft deferment and that he would play baseball in 1942. When the full story came out a short time later, Williams found himself at the center of another small scandal. The truth was that

In May 1941, private Hank Greenberg (in coat) enjoys a laugh with other soldiers at Fort Custer, Michigan. The Tigers all-star was one of many baseball players who joined the armed services during World War II.

Williams's status had been changed to 1-A by his Minnesota draft board—meaning that he would have been drafted—but the board's decision was appealed. This appeal went through the bureaucracy all the way up to Washington. Somewhere along the line Williams's status was changed back to 3-A. Williams publicly swore that all of this had been done by friends without his direct involvement; this was true, though only in the most technical sense of the word. Privately, those in Williams's camp tried to save his reputation by spreading stories about his difficult family situation; apparently, Williams had already committed a large part of his 1942 Red Sox salary to the care of his mother and worried that she would be left destitute if he joined the army at a small fraction of his baseball pay. When the Red Sox arrived in Florida for spring training, Williams's enemies in the press took aim and let loose with both barrels. Sportswriter Harold Kaese, one of Williams's most dedicated critics, wrote:

> *A youth, healthy and highly paid, is transferred from 3-A to 1-A by his local draft board. He is on the verge of being inducted into the Army, like thousands of other young men, like poor young men and rich young men, like Hank Greenberg, like [Senators shortstop] Cecil Travis, like Hugh Mulcahy. The case goes to Washington. There is a delay. Those with sensitive ears hear strings being pulled. An ominous silence envelops the youth. There is suspicion. There is contempt. There is hatred.*[1]

Other writers took sides for and against Williams. A nervous Boston front office privately urged Williams to enlist; he refused. In March two anonymous fans sent Williams blank sheets of yellow paper in the mail. Then, as the Red Sox and the rest of baseball settled into the familiar rituals of spring training, the Ted Williams draft controversy inexplicably faded away. Florida fans were forgiving; there was little of the expected booing and heckling. Boston third baseman Jim Tabor, who was to have taken Williams's place in the outfield, joked that "Roosevelt saw me shag flies for one day in left, and he gave Williams a deferment from the draft." Playing an early season series in New York, Williams was wildly cheered by a crowd that included thousands of newly-drafted soldiers. Apparently, more Americans wanted to see Ted Williams hit than see him fight. The Red Sox slugger further defused the issue when he assured reporters and friends that he would enlist as soon as the 1942 season ended. To Williams's credit, when he did join up he insisted, as did Hank Greenberg, on doing actual military service. Unlike may big leaguers who passed the war years playing baseball on military teams, Greenberg and Williams hardly picked up a bat or ball. Greenberg saw action in the Pacific with the Army Air Corps, and Williams took up the dangerous occupation of Marine Corps fighter pilot. Ted Williams later distinguished himself by serving a second time in the Korean War; he would lose most or all of five baseball seasons to wartime interruptions.

THE YEAR: 1942

The Yankees easily handled the loss of right fielder Tommy Henrich to the army in 1942, managing a near-repeat of their 1941 performance. With the powerful and versatile attack that characterized the Yankees throughout the 1930s, they led the AL in runs scored and fewest runs allowed. New York finished 103–51, nine games better than runner-up Boston. DiMaggio had an off year, batting .305 with 123 runs, 114 RBIs, 21 homers, and 13 triples. Outfielder Charlie Keller scored 106 runs, drove in 108, and drew 114 walks; sophomore shortstop Phil Rizzuto stole 22 bases, and his double-play partner Joe Gordon hit .322 with 103 RBIs, fourth-best in the AL. In a dramatic illustration of how disliked Ted Williams was by sportswriters, Gordon won the MVP vote, 270-249, despite leading the AL in strikeouts with 95 and errors at second base with 28; Williams not only batted .356 but won the Triple Crown with 36 home runs and 137 RBIs. Yankee pitchers Tiny Bonham, Spud Chandler, and Hank Borowy were second, third, and fifth in the AL in ERA at 2.27, 2.38, and 2.52. Bonham went 21–5 and was second in wins to Boston's Tex Hughson, who had a 22–6 record.

The 1942 NL race was a near-replay of 1941, as the St. Louis Cardinals fought a close battle with Brooklyn and won by two games. Foreshadowing many famous late-summer swoons to come, Brooklyn built a 10½ game lead by August but lost it all to a 43–8 Cardinals run. The 1942 Cards were one of the glories of Branch Rickey's legendary farm system. The team included home-grown products Stan Musial, who hit .315, second only to teammate Enos Slaughter's .318 and Ernie Lombardi's .330; shortstop Marty Marion, who led the league in doubles with 38; outfielder Terry Moore; and catcher Walker Cooper. Twenty-two game winner Mort Cooper, the NL MVP and ERA titlist at 1.78—who with Walker Cooper formed baseball's best brother battery— and 24-year-old Johnny Beazley, who was second to Cooper in wins with 21 and in ERA at 2.13, led the St. Louis pitching staff to a tiny team ERA of 2.55.

Brooklyn first baseman Dolph Camilli drove in 109 runs and hit 26 home runs, tied for second with the Giants Johnny Mize. Teammate Pete Reiser was third in hitting at .310 and first in stolen bases with 20. New York's Mel Ott launched a league-leading 30 homers with his patented bat-choking, drop-handed, uppercutting swing. He also led the NL in runs with 118 and walks with 109.

Veteran righty Red Ruffing won the opening game of the World Series 7-4, but St. Louis rallied to sweep the next four games. It was the first time New York had lost a post-season series since the 1926 Cardinals defeated them four games to three. St. Louis rookies

Stan Musial and Whitey Kurowski had key hits, but young starting pitcher Johnny Beazley was the surprise hero with a 2–0, 2.50 ERA performance. Another young pitcher, the 25-year-old Ernie White, defeated Chandler on a six-hit shutout in game three. The Cardinals turned in a staff ERA of 2.60 to the Yankees 4.50, while outscoring the Bronx Bombers 23 runs to 18.

Baseball felt the full brunt of the war in 1943. At Roosevelt's suggestion, many more night games were scheduled for the convenience of workers in war-related industries; for those working the lobster shift, some games were even played first thing in the morning. Nevertheless, attendance plummeted. In 1930 the major leagues as a whole had drawn over 10 million fans; the Great Depression had caused this to drop to about 6 million in 1934. World War II, however, hurt major-league baseball even more than the hard times of the 1930s. Attendance fell to a little under 3.7 million in 1943 and did not recover until the war ended. The Yankees led the AL by drawing 618,330 fans in 1943— roughly half of what they had drawn in 1930—and the St. Louis Browns attracted a measly 214,392 fans, or fewer than 3,000 per game. To put this in a modern perspective, in their first year the expansion Colorado Rockies of 1994 drew more fans than the entire American League in 1943. Today, it is not unusual for major-league clubs to sell more tickets in a week than the Browns did for an entire season during the war years. Wartime travel restrictions altered the baseball schedule and forced the big-league clubs to hold spring training in such glamorous play-spots as Wallingford, Connecticut (the Boston Braves), Cairo, Illinois (the St. Louis Cardinals), and French Lick, Indiana (the Chicago White Sox). Games were interrupted regularly by scheduled blackouts, and baseball radio broadcasters were forbidden to discuss weather conditions over the air in the unlikely case that they might aid enemy bombers. This led to one of the classic Dizzy Dean anecdotes. While broadcasting a Cardinals game that was being held up by rain, Dean told stories and stalled for a good hour, struggling to avoid mentioning the forbidden topic of weather. "If you folks don't know what's holding up this game," he finally blurted out, "just stick your head out the window." Remembering World War I, major-league baseball covered itself with the Stars and Stripes, initiating the now-traditional pregame playing of the National Anthem, making a show of deducting a portion of player's salaries to buy war bonds, and admitting uniformed servicemen and blood donors to games for free.

Just as World War II affected baseball, baseball affected the war in many small ways. Few American soldiers knew that their adversaries in the Pacific, the Japanese, also came from a baseball-playing nation. In a memoir of his war experiences, one American pilot recalled his shock at discovering this. While flying over Japanese-held territory on a bombing mission he noticed baseball fields, which somehow brought home to him the humanity of his enemy; until then he had never thought of the far-away objects of his bombs as fellow human beings. The Japanese, on the other hand, were very much aware of their connection to America through baseball. Although they had revered Babe Ruth since his celebrated visit to Japan in the 1930s—and nearly asked him to serve as a mediator during the peace talks that came at the end of the war—Japanese soldiers were known to shout "To Hell with Babe Ruth!" as they did battle with U.S. troops. To insult baseball's greatest player was to insult all of America. Former professional ballplayers saw military action on both sides. Some 425 American major leaguers, including 29 future Hall of Famers, lost at least one season to World War II. Some were killed; many never played again because of injury—the career of Washington's Cecil

Travis, for instance, was ended by frostbite suffered during the Battle of the Bulge—or because they were too old when they returned. Seventy-two veterans of the Japanese major leagues were killed fighting on the Japanese side. One of them, former 20-game winning pitcher Shinichi Ishimaru, died in the cockpit of a kamikaze plane. (Kamikaze planes were fitted with explosives and sent on suicide missions to crash intentionally into American warships; the pilots were not expected to survive.) Before he took off on his fatal flight, however, Ishimaru spoke a brief farewell to baseball and to life, got out a glove and a baseball and, after asking a newspaper reporter to serve as umpire, threw ten strikes to another navy man who was also an ex-ballplayer. Major-league second baseman Wayne Terwilliger recalled that after he and his fellow marines had defeated the Japanese on the island of Saipan after several days of incredibly bloody fighting, they celebrated by getting up two teams and playing a game of baseball in their muddy boots and torn battle fatigues. Cardinals outfielder Enos Slaughter, who also served on Saipan, remembered that games like these sometimes attracted a very unusual group of onlookers:

> You've heard what great baseball fans the Japanese are. Well, when we got to Saipan there were still quite a few of them holed up in the hills. I'll be damned if they didn't sneak out and watch us play ball. We could see them sitting there, watching the game. When it was over they'd fade back into their caves. But they could have got themselves killed for watching a ball game. Talk about real fans![2]

The subject of baseball comes up again and again in the battle lore of World War II. Many soldiers serving in Europe heard the rumor that the Germans had sent special agents, dressed as American GIs and speaking perfect American English, to infiltrate the American lines. When coming upon any such suspected agents, American soldiers were to test them by asking baseball questions that no red-blooded American boy would have any trouble answering, such as: "What was the Babe's lifetime average?" or "Who plays second for the Bums?" The theory was that no matter how thoroughly these spies might have studied America, only a real American could have absorbed the history, statistics, and vernacular of baseball. Later, this became a standard story component of B movies about the war.

Those on the American home front in World War II had to live with shortages of gasoline, tin, eggs, and many other materials that were needed to feed soldiers or to conduct the war effort. Many food items were rationed; artificial substitutes were developed for others. One example is the invention of oleomargarine as a substitute for butter. Though it is popular today under the name margarine, the original product was fairly nasty; colorless and with the consistency of Vaseline, it came in a plastic bag along with a packet of yellow food coloring that had to be added in and then massaged with the fingers until mixed in thoroughly.

The baseball equivalent of oleomargarine was a substance called balata. Created as an artificial substitute for rubber, balata replaced the rubber that made up part of the core of the major-league baseball and contributed significantly to its liveliness. Unfortunately, balata turned out to be about as lively as oleomargarine was appetizing; the first version of the balata ball was a complete failure and so dead that 11 of 1943's first 29 major-league games were won by shutouts. A second, slightly improved model was quickly introduced. Though it was tested and found to be over 25 percent less resilient than the ball of 1942, this was the baseball used by the two major leagues through 1945.

THE YEAR: 1943

Nearly every major-league team lost most of its key personnel to the armed forces in 1943. Baseball itself was allowed to continue because of its morale value, although Washington asked that games be scheduled for the maximum convenience of workers in war-related industries. That meant, among other things, more night games and the first twi-night double-headers. With wartime rubber rationing necessitating a deader baseball, big-league batting averages plummeted into the .240s.

The two clubs with the richest farm systems and the most talent before the war, the Yankees and Cardinals, handled the disruptions of wartime best and won pennants in 1943. The Cardinals replaced Enos Slaughter, Terry Moore, Johnny Beazley, and Howie Pollet with the likes of Lou Klein, Alpha Brazle, and Harry Brecheen. Walker Cooper hit .319 and Harry Walker .294, but St. Louis's biggest weapon was a blossoming 22-year-old hitter named Stan Musial, who, because of the large extended family that he supported, would not be drafted until 1945. The half-Polish, half-Czech son of a Pennsylvania steelworker, Musial led the NL in hitting at .357, triples with 20, doubles with 48, hits with 220, and total bases with 347. He also scored 108 runs (second only to Brooklyn's left-handed-hitting-short-stop-turned–third baseman Arky Vaughn), drove in a team-high 81 runs, and was voted NL MVP. St. Louis had the league's two top pitchers in Max Lanier, 15–7 with a 1.90 ERA, and Mort Cooper, 21–8 with the league's second-best ERA, 2.30. The Cardinals staff led the NL with a team ERA of 2.57, threw 21 shutouts, and struck out a league-best 639.

The Cincinnati Reds came in a distant second and Brooklyn finished third under new GM Branch Rickey. The pitching-poor Dodgers had the NL's strongest offense, led by the .330-hitting Billy Herman and outfielder Augie Galan, who drew a league-leading 103 walks. Chicago's Bill "Swish" Nicholson hit .309 and won two legs of the Triple Crown with 29 home runs and 128 RBIs. Pittsburgh's 36-year-old pitching ace Truett "Rip" Sewell pioneered the blooper pitch, which he nicknamed the "eephus," and went 21–9, the NL's best record. The blooper or eephus is an extremely slow breaking pitch that settles into the strike zone after sailing 15 feet or more into the air like a high-arc softball pitch. Accustomed to timing 85 MPH fastballs and 75 MPH curve balls, NL hitters practically screwed themselves into the ground swinging at and missing Sewell's slow stuff before it reached the plate. The owner of the perennially cellar-dwelling Philadelphia Phillies, Bill Cox, ran afoul of baseball's antigambling laws. Caught betting on his own team—to win, which some fans joked was the worse crime—Cox was banned from baseball and forced by Commissioner Landis to sell the team.

There was nothing new in the AL race, as the Yankees put 13½ games between themselves and runner-up Washington with a strong late-season drive. Thirty-six-year-old catcher Bill Dickey led the team in hitting at .351; Charlie Keller hit 31 home runs, second only to Tigers first baseman Rudy York's 34; and first baseman Nick Etten had 107 RBIs, second to York's 118. Thirty-two-year-old reserve infielder Frank Crosetti took over at shortstop, as Phil Rizzuto joined DiMaggio, Henrich, and Ruffing overseas. The Yankees 35-year-old ace, Spurgeon "Spud" Chandler, went 20–4 with a league-leading 1.64 ERA. Washington shortstop Luke Appling hit .328 to win the AL batting title vacated by the absent Ted Williams.

In the 1943 World Series, New York got its revenge for 1942 by winning easily in five games. Regular-season AL MVP Chandler was the pitching hero, winning games one and five 2-0 and recording an ERA of 0.50. Dickey was the batting hero of New York's tenth World

Championship, leading all hitters in RBIs and homering to account for both of the Yankees' runs in the series' final game.

Along with the newly deadened ball, the biggest changes in baseball were caused by the shortage of competent players, which reached an extreme between 1943 and 1945. In 1944 the formerly talent-rich St. Louis Cardinals, once the proud possessors of baseball's greatest farm system, actually ran a help-wanted ad in *The Sporting News*. "If you are a free agent and have previous professional experience," it began, "we may be able to place you on one of our clubs." As baseball historian Lee Allen wrote:

> *Players long forgotten reappeared on the major league scene. Others who never would be ready for the major leagues went through the motions of playing big league ball. Scouts no longer asked if a player could throw, run, and hit. They sought men with punctured ear-drums, epileptics, and mutes. The Cardinals introduced a pitcher considered highly desirable because as a baby he had swallowed a lump of coal and the subsequent operation to remove it left him unfit for military service. Cincinnati used a pitcher named Joe Nuxhall more than a month before his sixteenth birthday, the youngest player of all time.*[3]

Nuxhall—who was signed by a scout originally sent to try out Nuxhall's father, a 34-year-old semipro pitcher—was not an isolated case. A 16-year-old pitcher named Carl Scheib played for the Athletics, and Granville "Granny" Hamner played second base for the Phillies at 17. By 1945 there were 14 teenagers in the major leagues and 23 players 40 or older. Thirty-eight-

*Joe Nuxhall talks with Reds manager Bill McKechnie.
The 15-year-old pitcher joined the Reds in June 1944
and pitched one game before returning to high
school—with an ERA of 45.00.*

year-old Dodgers coach Leo Durocher activated himself
and immediately broke his hand trying to play second
base. Thirty-seven-year-old retired slugger Jimmie Foxx
took the mound for the Phillies and went 1–0 with a

1.59 ERA over nine games and 22⅔ innings. Pitcher Horace "Hod" Lisenbee, who had retired in 1936 with a record of 36–55, came back to pitch 31 games in relief for Cincinnati in 1945. At 47 years of age, Lisenbee was the last active major leaguer born in the nineteenth century. The 1945 St. Louis Browns created a sensation by signing 28-year-old outfielder Pete Gray. Not only had Gray lost virtually his entire right arm in a childhood accident, but Gray was a natural righty. Through sheer determination he had taught himself to hit with his left arm; and he threw and ran well enough to play a superb defensive outfield. Working his way up the minor-league ladder to Memphis of the Southern Association in 1943, in 1944 Gray batted .333, hit 5 homers, and stole a league-record 68 bases. He was voted league MVP. The Browns called him up the following year and he batted .218 with five stolen bases and two triples in 77 major-league games. That same year, 20 years after his major-league debut with the Pirates and seven years after his last full season, Hall of Famer Paul Waner tried to make the Yankees as an outfielder. "Hey Paul," one New York fan shouted to him during a game, "why are you in the outfield for the Yankees?" Waner shouted back: "Because Joe DiMaggio's in the fucking army."

As desperate as the major leagues were for talent during the war years, no team dared suggest doing away with the color line that had kept African-American players out of organized ball since the turn of the century. The same went for women baseball players, who, while clearly not in the same competitive class as the Negro Leaguers, were excluded from joining either the major or minor leagues by a similar unofficial ban that dated back to the case of female pitching sensation Jackie Mitchell, who was signed by the AA Chattanooga Lookouts and then, after striking out both Babe Ruth and Lou Gehrig in an exhibition game, was banned by

Commissioner Landis in 1931. Since then, it had been understood that no woman would be given a chance anywhere in organized baseball. In 1943, however, with baseball talent scarce and minor leagues dropping like flies, Cubs owner Philip Wrigley founded the All-American Girls Baseball League (AAGBL) with four all-female teams playing in Rockford, Illinois; South Bend, Indiana; Racine, Wisconsin; and Kenosha, Wisconsin. The AAGBL was a serious league; former major leaguers like Bill Wambsganss and Jimmie Foxx managed AAGBL clubs, and more than one son of an AAGBL player has played pro baseball. The mother of light-hitting 1980s utility infielder Casey Candaele, for example, was AAGBL star Helen Callahan St. Aubin, who stole 354 bases in her 388-game AAGBL career. The league as a whole drew very well, climbing from 176,000 paid admissions in 1943 to a peak of one million in 1948. Shortly after the war ended, however, public interest in women's baseball waned; the AAGBL folded during the 1950s. Today the league is commemorated by a special section of the National Baseball Hall of Fame in Cooperstown, New York, and by the 1992 film *A League of Their Own.*

The baseball played in the major leagues under wartime conditions could best be described as the return of dead ball, without the skill and finesse of the Ty Cobbs, Honus Wagners, Cy Youngs, or Christy Mathewsons. Total runs scored in the AL dropped from 5,902 in 1941 to 5,211 in 1942 and then to 4,796 in 1943. Home runs dipped from 734 to 533 to 473. The NL saw slightly less dramatic falloffs. Strange names like Hodgin, Case, Hopp, and Spence took the places of DiMaggio, Williams, Greenberg, and Reiser on batting-average leader boards. League stolen-base levels shot up from the 400s into the 500s and even into the 600s as those too weak, too slow, or too old to hit the balata ball over the fence struggled to generate offense. In

*Six players from the Kenosha and Racine AAGBL teams
pose before a June 1943 game.*

1945, the competitive low point of the war years, only
three AL batters hit over .300 and only one man, Browns
shortstop Vern Stephens, hit more than 18 homers.
While the old, the young, and the incompetent kept the
game going, the superstars of World War II–era baseball
were those with quirky injuries or ailments that allowed
them to play baseball but made military service impos-

sible. One example is Tigers pitcher Hal Newhouser, who suffered from a heart murmur; he won 54 games combined in 1944 and 1945 and was voted AL MVP both years. Another is Cleveland shortstop Lou Boudreau, who suffered from heel spurs; named the Indians player/manager at the age of 24 in 1942, Boudreau won the AL batting title in 1944 with a .327 average. Wartime baseball reached its lowest point in 1945, when the Detroit Tigers and the Chicago Cubs met in the World Series. Looking over a Detroit lineup that featured eight regulars with batting averages under .300—and one, shortstop Skeeter Webb, under .200—and a Chicago club that produced the amazing total of only 57 home runs playing in tiny Wrigley Field, one sportswriter described the matchup as "the fat men against the tall men at the office picnic." Asked for his pick, another replied: "I don't believe either club is capable of winning."

CHAPTER FOUR

The All-4F Infield: The AL Champion St. Louis Browns of 1944

In the National League, which was founded by Chicagoan William Hulbert in 1876, the St. Louis Cardinals were the last of the original eight franchises to win its first pennant. It took tremendous hitting seasons from Hall of Fame second baseman Rogers Hornsby and slugging first baseman Sunny Jim Bottomley and great pitching efforts from men of the caliber of Flint Rhem, Bill Sherdel, and Jesse Haines to bring St. Louis its first NL flag in 1926 after a half-century of failure. Coincidentally enough, St. Louis was last in the American League as well. One of the AL's eight founding clubs, the Browns had fielded winning teams in the early 1920s, the heyday of stars like George Sisler, Ken Williams, and Urban Shocker, but it also took them roughly 50 years to win their first pennant—from 1901 to 1944. The 1944 Browns, however, did not reach the top of the mountain by building a great dynasty or through record-breaking performances by superstar players. Rather than improving their club, the St. Louis Browns won by remaining more or less the same while

World War II and the military draft brought the rest of the AL down to their level. Featuring a weak lineup of George McQuinn, Don Gutteridge, Vern Stephens, Milt Byrne, and Chet Laabs and a mediocre pitching staff that boasted the likes of Steve Sundra, Bob Muncrief, Denny Galehouse, Nels Potter, and Al Hollingsworth, the 1943 Browns went 72–80 to finish 25 games off the pace of the already war-depleted New York Yankees. Fielding more or less the same personnel, the 1944 club went 89–65 and won the pennant.

A little-known historical footnote to the story of the 1944 Browns is the fact that they nearly won Los Angeles's first pennant instead of St. Louis's. Sixteen years before Walter O'Malley moved the Brooklyn Dodgers to the West Coast, Browns owner Donald Barnes, enticed by a sweetheart deal offered by Pacific Coast League mainstay Los Angeles, put together a deal that would have transferred his team to a new ballpark in Los Angeles. In St. Louis, the Browns struggled year-in and year-out to draw 150,000 fans for a season; in Los Angeles the team would be guaranteed half a million in annual ticket sales. Barnes had lined up the necessary support from his fellow owners and prepared a feasibility study that showed how a West Coast team could be added without disrupting the AL travel schedule. His only mistake was timing. The formal vote that would allow him to make the move to Los Angeles was scheduled for December 8, 1941—one day after the Japanese attack on Pearl Harbor. Needless to say, that vote was never taken.

Even if they were the least affected of all AL clubs by the draft, the Brownies epitomized the ragged state of wartime baseball. They had nine players 34 years of age or older and history's first-ever all-4F infield. Given to those with serious physical or other disabilities, 4F was the lowest draft classification; someone rated 4F was at the very bottom of the list of potential draftees. The Browns had only one player with more than 11 home runs and only one with a batting average over .300—outfielder Mike Kreevich, who was just over at .301. Manager Luke Sewell, a former major-league catcher and the brother of former Indians shortstop Joe Sewell, pinch-hit, pinch-ran, and switched players in and out of the starting lineup with dizzying frequency and with remarkable success. It seemed as though Sewell had a sixth sense for how a particular player would perform in a particular role at a particular time. Midway through the Browns' championship season of 1944, when Washington sportswriter Shirley Povich asked Sewell, "What's going on here, Luke? You change these line-ups every day! You must smell these guys on the bench getting hot," Sewell replied: "No, Shirley, I smell those bums out there on the field getting cold." On top of their other problems, many of the St. Louis Browns of 1944 drank too much, especially pitcher Sig Jackucki, pitcher Tex Shirley, and outfielder Mike Kreevich—the man who in 1945 would lose his job to one-armed Pete Gray.

How bad were the Browns before 1944? The franchise bottomed out in 1939 when it lost 111 games and came in 64½ games back of New York. In the four years between 1940 and 1943, the Browns averaged 25 games out and fifth place in the standings. Even counting the pennant season of 1944, they drew an incredibly low total of 3,330,861 fans for the entire decade; in 1941, fewer than 200,000 fans saw the Browns play. Not that they were much better than that after 1944; the Browns followed up their championship season by finishing sixth or seventh seven times before giving up and moving to Baltimore for the 1954 season. As the modern Baltimore Orioles, the club has had a very different history.

Dividing the failures of the 1930s from the failures of the late 1940s and early 1950s was the club's one, shining moment of glory. Led by 23-year-old slugging shortstop Vern Stephens, who hit .293 with 20 home runs and a league-high 109 RBIs, .295-hitting outfielder

Milt Byrnes, and Kreevich, the Browns offense scored a respectable 684 runs. Their pitching was not too bad, either; old Nels Potter and young Jack Kramer won 19 and 17 games respectively. The staff was rounded out by Bob Muncrief, Denny Galehouse, and a 34-year-old dark horse named Sig Jackucki. Jackucki was a classic product of wartime baseball. A 0–3 lifetime pitcher who had failed miserably in a brief major-league trial and retired in 1939, Jackucki was rediscovered in 1944 in a Houston, Texas, factory league and given a spot in the Browns rotation; he went 13–9 with a 3.55 ERA. This team shocked the baseball world and set an AL record by winning the first nine games of the 1944 season. By September, however, the 9–0 start was just a memory; the Browns were involved in a tight, four-team race. Unable to absorb the losses of pitcher Tex Hughson and infielder Bobby Doerr, the Boston Red Sox dropped out of contention, leaving St. Louis, Detroit, and New York in a neck-and-neck race down to the wire.

Notwithstanding his comical name and meager baseball resume, Jackucki was no joke to the New York Yankees or the Detroit Tigers after his thirteenth victory gave St. Louis the pennant after a series of bitterly fought September battles. On September 29, St. Louis had knocked the Yankees out of contention with a double-header sweep, followed by another win the next day. Detroit won two out of three from Washington to drop into a tie with the Browns for first place. Then, on the final day of the season, Tigers 27-game winner and league ERA-leader Dizzy Trout lost to the Senators. Meanwhile, two homers by Chet Laabs and another by Vern Stephens gave the Browns a victory over New York that clinched the pennant by one game over Detroit. The Browns .578 winning percentage tied the existing record for the lowest winning percentage by a pennant-winner in major-league history. That record had been set by the 1926 St. Louis Cardinals.

THE YEAR: 1944

The St. Louis Cardinals won the NL pennant to make the 1944 World Series a one-city affair. This was baseball's first, last, and only all–St. Louis championship series and appropriately, it bore no resemblance to a New York–style subway series. As owners of St. Louis's only baseball park, Sportsman's Park, the Browns were the Cardinals' landlords; this meant that the distinction between road and home games was lost because all series games were played in the same facility. Things also got complicated for the two managers, Billy Southworth of the Cards and Luke Sewell of the Browns. Like a lot of major leaguers who played in two-team cities, Southworth and Sewell saved money by sharing an apartment. After all, the NL Cardinals and the AL Browns were never at home at the same time. It had certainly not occurred to them that their teams might meet in October. When the unthinkable happened, the two managers took turns sleeping on the couch. Unfortunately, there is no record of their dinner-table conversations during the series. With no travel days, the Cardinals took the six-game series in six days, but the underdog Browns put up a good fight. The Browns' collection of semipros and misfits outpitched the Cardinals and their staff of real pitchers like Mort Cooper, Harry Brecheen, and Max Lanier, but Jackucki and company were let down by poor hitting and fielding. Second baseman Don Guterridge and shortstop Vern Stephens made three errors apiece, and the Browns team committed a total of ten errors to their opponents' one.

The 1944 NL pennant race was a routine affair, as the Cardinals won their third-straight pennant behind respectable ballplayers like Marty Marion, Walker Cooper, Johnny Hopp, and Stan Musial, who hit .347 with 112 runs and a league-leading 51 doubles. In the AL, however, the acute shortage of players led to an

*In 1944, manager Luke Sewell led the lowly
St. Louis Browns to the franchise's sole
American League pennant.*

unlikely pennant for the perennial doormat Browns, a
team that had finished in the second division nine out
of the previous ten seasons. The club had never before
won a pennant in 43 years of AL competition and had
lost 111 games as recently as 1939.

The sportswriters couldn't bring themselves to name one of the Browns AL MVP, so the award went to Detroit Tigers ace left-hander Hal Newhouser, who had a record of 29–9. Newhouser and teammate Paul "Dizzy" Trout were first and second in wins and ERA. Cleveland's Lou Boudreau took the batting title at .327 and New York's Nick Etten led in homers with 22. The NL MVP award went to Cardinals shortstop Marty Marion. MVP runner-up Swish Nicholson of the Cubs had another big power-hitting year, producing an NL-high 33 homers and 122 RBIs. Cincinnati's wartime search for talent reached an extreme when they plucked 15-year-old pitcher Joe Nuxhall out of high school to pitch one game in the big leagues; he returned to his studies with a major-league ERA of 45.00.

A month after the 1944 World Series, baseball's 78-year-old commissioner Kenesaw Mountain Landis died. His 35-year tenure was characterized by a strong and successful stand against gambling-related corruption and by surprising flashes of sympathy for the players' side in disputes with owners. On many other issues, however, including the maintenance of baseball's color line, Landis toed the owners' line. From 1944 on, the baseball owners have made sure never to give any other commissioner anything resembling the power that they came to regret giving to Landis. He was replaced in 1945 by the harmless former Kentucky governor and U.S. senator Albert "Happy" Chandler, who would be fired after a single seven-year term.

CHAPTER FIVE

Down to the Wire: The Classic Pennant Races of the 1940s

Despite the upheavals of the war years and the strange effects of the balata ball in the middle years of the decade, the years 1940 to 1948 saw some of the most exciting pennant races ever. If you made a list of the best 10 or 15 races of the twentieth century, as many as half of them took place during those nine years. The best of the best were the AL races of 1940 and 1948—two multiteam races that remained unsettled until the final day—and the NL races of 1941, 1942, and 1946, all of which matched two of the all-time greatest NL dynasties: the St. Louis Cardinals and their great Rickey-built farm system against the team Branch Rickey took over in 1942, the Brooklyn Dodgers.

The 1940 Cleveland Indians had a problem. It certainly was not any lack of playing talent. The team boasted a deep pitching staff that included Bob Feller, Al Milnar, Mel Harder, Al Smith, and Johnny Allen; a fine defense anchored by shortstop Lou Boudreau and third baseman Ken Keltner; and a consistent if not intimidating offense that featured slugging first baseman

Hal Trosky and team RBI-leader Boudreau. The Indians' problem was sour-faced manager Ossie Vitt, who had taken over for Steve O'Neill before the 1938 season. Born Oscar Joseph Vitt in San Francisco, California, Vitt was a survivor of the dead-ball era. A physically small, lifetime .238 hitter who had played third base for the Red Sox and Tigers in the 1910s, a time when third basemen were judged by how they defended the bunt rather than by how many home runs they hit, Vitt had the kind of scrappy aggressiveness that is often mistaken for strong leadership by those who hire managers. Unfortunately, 1940 was a long time after 1917. What may have been a standard motivating tactic to Vitt sounded to his players like nagging; when Vitt browbeat and chewed his players out verbally, the way John McGraw might have done—and gotten away with—they chewed right back. The team had finished third under Vitt in 1938 and in 1939, but Cleveland fans were beginning to think that the Indians were good enough to contend for the AL pennant. Under the pressure of increased expectations, Vitt got worse. He unnerved the team by pacing the dugout, muttering and cursing under his breath. While coaching third base during one game he turned to the opposing dugout and said of one of his players: "How am I supposed to win with a bum like that?" On one rainy day Trosky joked that he might be risking pneumonia by going out to play. Vitt answered him: "Why don't you [go out and play anyway]? You're not doing us any good."

The last straw came on June 11, when Vitt lost his composure after a 9-2 Bob Feller loss to the Red Sox. "Look at him," Vitt barked, "He's supposed to be my ace. How am I supposed to win a pennant with that kind of pitching?" In 1940 Feller would compile a record of 27 wins, 11 losses, and a 2.61 ERA; he would lead the AL in wins, games, starts, complete games, innings pitched, strikeouts, and shutouts. The following day the Indians lost another game to Boston, their

*Cleveland Indians manager Ossie Vitt
encourages one of his players during a
1938 spring-training game. A players' rebellion
led to Vitt's dismissal after the 1940 season.*

eighth defeat in their previous 13 games. Cleveland was
now two games off the pace in a tight, four-team race
that also included the Red Sox, Yankees, and Detroit
Tigers. The Indians' veterans decided that they had had

enough; a group including Feller, Trosky, Keltner, and eight or nine others marched into the office of team president Alva Bradley and demanded that Vitt be fired. Bradley refused, but promised instead to fire Vitt after the season. Soon, however, word of the Indians' players mutiny was leaked to the press and stories appeared that portrayed the players as crybabies and Vitt as a martyr to the selfishness of spoiled, modern ballplayers. Many of the players involved in the protest were booed for the rest of the season by Cleveland fans, while Vitt was enthusiastically cheered whenever he walked onto the field. Any further crisis was defused when the players appeared to back down by issuing a public letter of apology.

Although the Indians players appeared to be the losers in the "crybabies" episode, the affair had its positive effects. One was that the team seemed to pull together; in the several weeks following their letter of apology, the Indians went on a winning roll and held first place by several games in mid-August. The other was that the players ignored Vitt and more or less managed the games by themselves, inserting pinch-hitters, putting on plays, and paying little attention to Vitt's signs. Then in September the race began to tighten. With eight games to go in the 1940 season, the Tigers and Indians were tied at 85–61; to add to the drama and suspense, six of the two teams' remaining eight games were against each other. "There hasn't been anything like this since 1908," said A's manager Connie Mack, "when the same two teams went down to the last day." The Indians faltered; they lost two of three in Detroit and then split a pair with the lowly St. Louis Browns. Many blamed Vitt for having overused team ace Bob Feller, who was now pitching out of the bullpen between starts and was well on his way to an arm-wearying 320-inning season. Meanwhile, Detroit swept a doubleheader from the White Sox; first baseman

Rudy York won game one with a tenth-inning double, and Hank Greenberg's 41st home run (and 150th RBI) in the seventh inning tied game two. The Tigers won that game 3-2 on York's eighth-inning sacrifice fly. When Detroit arrived in Cleveland for a season-ending three-game series, they were two games ahead and needed only a single victory to clinch the AL pennant.

With Feller scheduled to pitch the first game of the series—in Cleveland—Indians fans were confident. They were also eager to get even with the many Tigers fans who had chanted "crybabies" at their players in Detroit and pelted them with fruit and eggs. Upon the Tigers' arrival by train at Cleveland's Union Station, a crowd of several hundred splattered Greenberg, Gehringer, and company with a barrage of tomatoes and rotten apples. Another thing in the Indians' favor was the fact that Detroit's September charge had left veteran pitchers Bobo Newsom, Tommy Bridges, and Schoolboy Rowe thoroughly exhausted. It was Rowe's turn to pitch in game one of the series, but 30 minutes before game time Rowe told manager Del Baker that he could not go. Faced with a choice between four young-sters—the 9–9 Hal Newhouser, the 3–7 Dizzy Trout, the 3–7 Fred Hutchinson, and the 2–0 Floyd Giebell—Baker summoned the team's eight regular position play-ers and put it to a vote. The 30-year-old Giebell, who had pitched the fewest major-league innings in 1940 but who had the most minor-league experience, got seven votes and was sent to the bullpen to warm up.

In a game punctuated by showers of bottles and other garbage aimed at the Tigers players and a fistfight between an abusive Cleveland fan and Detroit catcher George "Birdie" Tebbetts, Giebell and Feller held the hitters scoreless until the fourth, when Tigers slugger Rudy York lofted a harmless-looking fly ball down the left-field line that caught a gust of wind and barely drifted over the fence at the 320-foot mark. York's homer, which made the score 2-0, turned out to be the difference, as Giebell silenced the Indians' bats with a complete-game, six-hit shutout. Feller also pitched a complete game, allowing only three hits, but it did not matter; the Tigers were going to the World Series and the Indians were staying home. Curiously, this game was the last hurrah for many of the men involved. Despised by his players, Cleveland manager Vitt was fired soon after and never coached or managed another major-league game. Detroit skipper Del Baker did his best to annoy the Tigers as well, by crowing to the press about how brilliant he had been to start Giebell when in fact he had been unable to make a decision and had passed the buck to his players. Baker managed Detroit for two more seasons, finishing fourth and fifth, but he was gone by the time most of the Tigers regulars returned from military service. A September addition to the Indians staff, Giebell was ineligible to pitch in the 1940 World Series, which the Tigers lost to the Cincinnati Reds in seven games; he came back the following season, but went 0–0 with a 6.03 ERA before returning to the minors. Floyd Giebell never won another big-league game.

Connie Mack may have called 1940 a repeat of 1908, but the wild and crazy AL race of 1948 was even more so. Sparked by Joe DiMaggio's epic season, the New York Yankees had run away with the 1941 pennant. Then came the war years, when baseball rosters were turned upside down and inside out. In the NL, the deep Cardinals and Dodgers organizations fought it out for most of the wartime pennants; the AL flags were won by impostors wearing New York pinstripes or Detroit orange and black, or by collections of undraftable mediocrities like the St. Louis Browns. By 1947 and 1948, however, DiMaggio and Williams and Feller were back from the war and the AL balance of power had returned to something resembling prewar normalcy; the Yankees, Red Sox, Tigers, and Indians were up, and the White Sox, Athletics, Senators, and Browns were down.

By midseason of 1948 Detroit had dropped off the pace, replaced in contention by a flash-in-the-pan Philadelphia club that plummeted from second place at the All-Star break to fourth place, 12½ games out, at the season's end. New York, Boston, and Cleveland took the race for the AL flag down to the season's final three days. Led by Joe DiMaggio, who hit .320 with a league-leading 39 homers and 155 RBIs, and Tommy Henrich, who enjoyed a career year, the Yankees were explosive. Their pitching, however, was weakened by injuries to team ace Allie Reynolds and fellow starter Frank "Spec" Shea. On Labor Day, Boston, New York, and Cleveland were separated by a mere 1½ games. The Yankees were good enough to win 94 games but were eliminated on the next-to-last day of the season by a loss to the Red Sox. The Indians led Boston by one game on the morning of the final day of the 1948 season, but Bob Feller lost yet another clutch game, 7-1 to Detroit's Hal Newhouser. The Red Sox, meanwhile, demolished the Yankees for the second day in a row, by a score of 10-5. With the Indians and Red Sox ending the season in a flat-footed tie—something that had never occurred before in AL history—league officials consulted their rules and found that the AL flag was to be decided by a one-game playoff, with the site determined by a coin toss. Boston won and the playoff was set for Fenway Park.

The Red Sox were managed by Joe McCarthy, who came out of retirement two years after leaving the Yankees in mid-1946. The club featured the great Ted Williams, who won the AL batting title at .369 and drove in 127 runs; a double-play combination of Bobby Doerr and Vern Stephens, who combined for an awesome 56 homers and 258 RBIs; and an excellent pitching staff of Joe Dobson, Mel Parnell, Jack Kramer, Ellis Kinder, and Denny Galehouse. In a season that eerily parallels the 1978 duel between Boston and New York, the Red Sox were baseball's comeback kids. The club was a miserable 14–23 on Memorial Day. After streaking into first place, the Red Sox blew a late-season lead of five games; they had to win the final two games of the season to force a playoff.

Starting with their colorful owner Bill Veeck, the Cleveland Indians were one of baseball's classic collections of characters, including dominant pitchers Bob Lemon and Bob Feller; shortstop, manager, and RBI-man Lou Boudreau; team vice president and former Detroit Tigers slugger Hank Greenberg; and the AL's first African-American player, outfielder Larry Doby. Veeck was known for his outrageous and creative promotions, which boosted attendance everywhere he went. In Cleveland Veeck selected a "Mr. Average Fan," a man named "Good Old Joe" Earley, and periodically showered him with gifts; he hired roving barbers to give fans haircuts during games; and he built a ballpark nursery for the convenience of fans who happened to be mothers with small children. Occasionally, Veeck went a little too far, as when he signed a midget named Eddie Gaedel, gave him the number ⅛, and put him into a game; not surprisingly, Gaedel walked. In 1948 Veeck secretly moved the Indians' outfield fences in and out before each home series, depending on the team's opponent. Some of his tactics were designed to serve both a public relations and a baseball purpose. One example is Veeck's signing of former Negro League pitching great Satchel Paige to an Indians contract in June 1948. Paige had once been a great fastball pitcher, but now he was chiefly famous for his slow breaking stuff and his arsenal of hilarious stories. The Brooklyn Dodgers had broken the baseball color line the year before by signing shortstop Jackie Robinson, but this

Owner Bill Veeck (center) celebrates the Indians 1948 World Series victory with shortstop and manager Lou Boudreau (right) and coach Bill McKechnie.

had not led to an immediate rush by major-league clubs to sign other African-Americans. Some clubs simply refused to integrate; others were cautious, scouting only young Negro League players on the theory that they might have to go through an adjustment period or some time in the minors and that, therefore, there was no point in signing a player much over 30 years old. For both reasons, many in baseball were outraged when Veeck signed Paige, who was then well past 40—his exact age remains unknown—and on the downside of his Negro League career. Veeck was accused by the press of pulling a cheap publicity stunt and cruelly exploiting an old man. "To sign a hurler at Paige's age is to demean the standards of baseball," thundered *The Sporting News,* "Further complicating the situation is the suspicion that if Satchel were white, he would not have drawn a second thought from Veeck." Incredibly, the voice of organized baseball, an institution that had maintained a tradition of strict Jim Crowism for decades, was accusing Veeck of racism because he signed an African-American player. As it turned out, Paige worked 72⅔ innings of quite effective relief and compiled a decidedly undemeaning record of 6–1 with a 2.48 ERA. Veeck made *The Sporting News* eat its words. After each successful Paige outing, Veeck sent the newspaper a telegram something like the following: NINE INNINGS. FOUR HITS. FIVE STRIKEOUTS. WINNING PITCHER: PAIGE. DEFINITELY IN LINE FOR THE SPORTING NEWS AWARD AS ROOKIE OF THE YEAR.[1]

The big suspense going into the one-game 1948 AL playoff was who was going to start. Both managers were coy, refusing to name a starter until the last possible moment; and both made strange choices. With most of his staff tired, Joe McCarthy asked catcher Tebbetts for his opinion on who should pitch. Tebbetts suggested Tex Hughson, a once-dominant right-hander who had only recently recovered from serious arm trouble. McCarthy rejected that choice and then polled the entire pitching staff; each man nominated himself. Finally, McCarthy picked righty Denny Galehouse, a 36-year-old reliever. Galehouse had only an 8–7 record, but he was considered mentally tough and, unlike most of the Boston staff, he was thoroughly rested. The Red Sox had the 16–10 Dobson, the 18–5 Kramer, and the 10–7 Kinder, but the obvious choice would have been lefty Mel Parnell, who had a record of

15–8 and who had not pitched in three days. The choice of Galehouse reminded some of the Red Sox players of Connie Mack's brilliant and courageous selection of Howard Ehmke as the starter for game one of the 1929 World Series. To play with the Indians' heads, McCarthy kept his choice of Galehouse secret right up until game time. On the Cleveland side, player/manager Lou Boudreau was doing the same thing. He tried to put the decision up to a player vote, but second baseman Joe Gordon insisted that the club would line up 100 percent behind whomever Boudreau picked. Boudreau decided on Gene Bearden, but he did not tell anyone. All season long, Boudreau had made it a habit of placing a new baseball in the locker of his starter for that day. Before this game, he frustrated a clubhouse spy sent by Joe McCarthy to find out the Cleveland starter by placing new, white baseballs in several pitchers' lockers. When the game began, the Red Sox were surprised to see Bearden warming up to pitch. Bearden may have won 20 games and the AL ERA title in 1948, but he was a risky choice for two reasons: one, he was a left-hander—with its short left-field wall, topped by a screen to catch home-run balls, Fenway Park is traditionally death on left-handed pitching—and two, he was a rookie.

The game itself was an anticlimax. Galehouse did not have his control and gave up two home runs into the left-field screen by Boudreau and Keltner. Boudreau added another homer off Ellis Kinder and the Indians won, 6-3. As for Bearden, he was in top form, keeping the Red Sox' sluggers off balance with an assortment of knuckleballs, change-ups, and curve balls. He struck out six and scattered five hits. Afterward, many Boston players and fans second-guessed McCarthy for pitching Galehouse, but Ted Williams knew that anyone can win a one-game playoff; he attributed Cleveland's victory to

71

the great season turned in by Lou Boudreau. In his 1969 autobiography *My Turn at Bat,* Williams wrote of 1948:

> *Lou Boudreau did everything for the Indians but drive the bus that year. He managed great, he worked with the pitchers great, he played great position at shortstop, he hit for average and he drove in runs. I've never seen clutch hitting like he did that year. Boudreau was a hell of a player, boy. One of the greatest seasons in American League history was Lou Boudreau's 1948 season.*[2]

The sportswriters agreed; they voted Boudreau, who besides hitting .355 with 18 homers and 106 RBIs also led the league in double plays and fielding average, AL MVP by 109 points over runners-up Joe DiMaggio and Ted Williams.

THE YEAR: 1945

In July and August the American League pennant race was beginning to look like a repeat of 1944, with Washington, New York, St. Louis, and Detroit all in contention. Things changed, however, as major leaguers began to return one by one from overseas. Charlie Keller returned to the Yankees, Feller to the Indians, and Appling to the White Sox. Slugger Hank Greenberg came back with the biggest bang, picking up and carrying a weak Tigers team to the AL flag.

Throughout Hank Greenberg's career, the Detroit Tigers seemed to rise and fall in the standings along with Greenberg's individual performances. In 1934 Detroit won the pennant and Greenberg hit 63 doubles and batted .339. The next year he hit 36 homers, drove in 170 runs, and hit .328; Detroit won again and Greenberg was voted the unanimous MVP. In 1936,

Lou Boudreau poses in the Indians dugout in 1948, the year that he led his team to a World Series championship. Boudreau received that year's AL MVP award.

after losing Greenberg to injury, Detroit finished 19½ games out. In 1940 Greenberg won his second MVP award, and his 50 doubles, 41 homers, and 150 RBIs paced Detroit to another pennant. Perhaps even more indicative of Greenberg's greatness, however, is the quality of his off seasons. In 1939, for example, he fell off to a .312 average with 33 home runs and 112 RBIs—numbers that a Reggie Jackson or a Jose Canseco would be proud of.

Greenberg left Detroit for the army 19 games into the 1941 campaign, not to return until July 1, 1945. He homered in his first game back against Philadelphia and then began the painful process of playing himself back into shape. By mid-September, Detroit had a 1½ game lead after taking three of five from second-place Washington and their all-knuckleballing pitching staff. As in 1944, the pennant race came down to a crucial series between Detroit and St. Louis. With Detroit needing one win to clinch the AL flag, 26-year-old Virgil Trucks, just three days out of the Navy, started for Detroit in game one; 15–11 Nels Potter took the mound for St. Louis. With the Tigers up 2-1, Detroit ace Hal Newhouser relieved in the sixth and narrowly escaped a bases-loaded, one-out situation; in the seventh, however, he allowed the tying and go-ahead runs. The score remained 3-2 in the ninth, when lead-off man Hub Walker, pinch-hitting for Newhouser, walked and light-hitting Skeeter Webb bunted his way on. After another bunt moved both runners into scoring position, the right-handed Potter walked left-handed-hitting Doc Cramer to load the bases and go for the double play with Greenberg, but Greenberg did not cooperate, clouting his eleventh career grand slam to win the game and the pennant for Detroit. In 270 at bats, or less than half of a season, the 34-year-old Greenberg had scored 47 runs and driven in 60 runs on 35 extra-base hits and a .311 batting average.

On the same page as Hank Greenberg in most baseball encyclopedias can be found Pete Gray, who played 77 games for the 1945 Browns, batting .218 with six doubles and two triples, to become one of the most celebrated disabled players in major-league history. Despite his mediocre stats, Gray was no publicity stunt; lacking virtually all of his right arm, Gray had hit .333 with 68 stolen bases to become MVP of the Southern Association in 1944. In the end, Gray was undone by big-league off-speed pitching, but there have been other disabled players who found success in the major leagues: men like Hugh "One-arm" Daily, who won 73 big-league games and threw a no-hitter, and the most successful of all, Hall of Famer Mordecai "Three-finger" Brown, who compiled a 2.06 ERA over 14 seasons and attributed the unpredictable break of his famous curveball to the deformed and missing fingers on his throwing hand.

The greatest NL pennant races of the early and middle 1940s were the three magnificent battles waged by the Brooklyn Dodgers against the St. Louis Cardinals in 1941, 1942, and 1946. Both teams were throwbacks to the 1930s, full of hard-drinking tough guys and bean-ball artists. Brooklyn got its personality from its manager, ex–Gas House Gang figure Leo "The Lip" Durocher; the powerful Dolph Camilli, a muscular home-run hitting first baseman and team leader; the slick and ultrapro-fessional former Cub second baseman Billy Herman; the hard-bitten ex-Cardinal outfielder Joe Medwick; and Fred "Dixie" Walker, a favorite of Brooklyn's tough, working-class fans who was given the unique Brooklynese nickname "The Peeple's Cherce." Ex-Cardinal Mickey Owen handled the catching. The Dodgers lineup was rounded out by a pair of 22-year-olds: outfielder Pete Reiser and shortstop Harold "Pee Wee" Reese. As youngsters Reiser and Reese were bullied and hazed by their teammates until Camilli put a stop to it. "Leave those kids alone," Camilli said, "They're going to help us win the pennant." To give an idea of what it was like to be a young player trying to break into a team like the Dodgers, Reiser once told a reporter how grateful he felt toward pitcher Whitlow Wyatt for being nice to him. When the reporter asked what Wyatt had done, Reiser replied: "He said 'Hello' to me." In a way, Reiser was another ex-Cardinal. He had been the pride of Branch Rickey's vast St. Louis organization until Commissioner Landis released him along with several dozen fellow minor-leaguers in one of Landis's periodic attacks on the concept of the farm system. Reiser was picked up as a free agent by Brooklyn for $200. Like many of his teammates, Reiser was a little too aggressive. After a brilliant start, his baseball career was ultimately ruined by head injuries suffered in several terrible collisions with the unpadded outfield walls of NL parks. The Brooklyn pitchers, led by staff aces Kirby Higbe and Wyatt, were—like all pitchers who wanted to get along with Leo Durocher—ready and willing to knock down or even bean opposing batters.

The Cardinals of 1941 were just as tough, and if anything, more talented than the Dodgers. The team was managed by Billy Southworth, who once said, when told that Durocher had refused to pose with him for a pregame photograph: "I'm out to beat him and he's out to beat me. So why pose in front of the public smiling and shaking hands when we don't feel that way at all?" Playing first base was Johnny Mize, a physically imposing left-handed home-run hitter who was amazingly difficult to strike out. Mize hit 359 career home runs with only 524 strikeouts; three times he performed the feat of recording fewer strikeouts than homers. At shortstop was Hall of Fame gloveman Marty Marion. The outfield was manned by aggressive base-stealer Enos "Country" Slaughter, Terry Moore, and leadoff man Johnny Hopp. The tough St. Louis pitching staff included lefty Ernie White; veteran right-hander Lon Warneke; and Mort Cooper, whose brother Walker shared the catching job with Gus Mancuso.

These two teams fought to a virtual draw in early August. Through late August and into the first half of September they took turns in first and second place, with neither club falling farther than two games off the pace. With the Cardinals hanging tough despite injuries to Slaughter, Mize, Moore, and both Cooper brothers, the pennant race came down to one wild, 17-day road trip by the Brooklyn Dodgers. The trip, which was punctuated by several beanball incidents, nasty confrontations with umpires, and a warning from NL president Ford Frick, included a pennant-deciding series against the Cardinals in St. Louis. Brooklyn arrived in St. Louis in first place by one game. Durocher picked ancient knuckleballer Freddie Fitzsimmons to start game one against Ernie White. A thickset, short-tempered man who later served as a general manager in the NFL, Fitzsimmons has been very underrated by posterity despite a fine career record of 217–146; his nickname, "Fat Freddie" may have something to do with it. Fitzsimmons's start was, as Durocher later said, "one of those games." In the eighth inning of a scoreless tie, Reiser faked an attempt to steal home and caused a surprised White to balk, but umpire Al Barlick refused to make the call, saying, "I'm not going to let you win a game as important as this on a technicality." Durocher went crazy. In the bottom of the inning, with Johnny Mize up and two on and two out, Durocher tried to take his pitcher out, but Fitzsimmons, who absolutely despised Mize, refused to go. Talking loud enough for Mize to hear, the Dodger pitcher growled: "That picklehead ain't going to hit me. I'll knock his cap off." The next pitch whizzed, as advertised, by Mize's ear. Durocher could hardly bear to watch what came next. With the likely winning run on third base, Fitzsimmons alternated knuckleballs for strikes with vicious knockdown pitches—each of which he announced in a loud voice— that catcher Owen barely managed to catch, until the count ran to 3-2. Fitzsimmons then glared at Mize, snarled, "It's gonna be right where you like it, tomato-face, and you're never going to get the bat off your shoulder," and let loose a big, tantalizing slow curve. Mize double and triple-clutched, but could not pull the trigger; the pitch floated across the plate for strike three and the inning was over. The Dodgers went on to win the game in 11 innings.

Despite the Cardinals' late-season addition of the 20-year-old Stan Musial, who batted .426 over 12 games in September, the Dodgers won 100 games and their first NL pennant since 1920, thanks to an MVP season from Camilli, who hit a league-best 34 home runs and drove in 120 runs, and matching 22-win seasons from Wyatt and Higbe. St. Louis won 97 and finished 2½ games out.

Things turned out differently in 1942, mainly because Stan Musial was around for the entire pennant race. As late as the third and fourth weeks of August, however, Brooklyn looked like a sure bet to repeat. In July, Pete Reiser, who was batting .383, fractured his skull against an outfield fence while trying to catch a fly ball hit by Country Slaughter; Reiser returned to play against doctor's orders but, suffering from double vision and headaches, he slumped to .310. He never played at the top of his game again. Still, the Dodgers led by 10½ games going into a mid-August doubleheader versus the Cardinals. A few days earlier, team president Larry MacPhail gathered the team together and warned them: "I'm telling you, boys, the Cardinals are going to beat you if you're not careful. You guys are getting lackadaisical, you think you have it clinched, and before you know it, they are going to beat you out."[3] Taking their cue from the team's hard-playing, hard-partying manager, Leo Durocher, the Dodgers were not careful.

The first sign that MacPhail might be a prophet came when St. Louis swept both games of the doubleheader and then started on a winning roll. Led by the hitting of Slaughter and Musial along with the MVP pitching of Mort Cooper, who would finish the season with a record of 22–7 and a league-leading ERA of 1.78, the Cardinals put on an almost unbelievable run of 43–8 in their last 51 games. The Dodgers tried to fight back—winning the final eight games of the season—but they could not keep pace with a St. Louis juggernaut that won 10 of its last 11. The Dodgers lost first place for good on September 13 and finished second, 2 games out, despite winning 104 games. As it turned out, the disappointing pennant loss of 1942 would, indirectly, change the course of baseball history. Heartbroken after losing the 1941 World Series and the 1942 pennant, Brooklyn's brilliant but hotheaded team president, Larry MacPhail, quit baseball and joined the army. The man Brooklyn hired to take his place was St. Louis's Branch Rickey.

The 1946 NL race began with the coining of an immortal baseball quotation. Handicapping the NL race with a group of reporters before an early-season game against New York, Brooklyn manager Leo Durocher dismissed the Giants' chances with a remark something like "All nice guys. They'll finish last." Taken out of context and slightly rewritten, Durocher's words appeared in the next day's newspaper as "Nice guys finish last"—an apt summation of Durocher's baseball philosophy that would later serve as the title for Durocher's 1975 autobiography. Incidentally, Mel Ott, Johnny Mize, and the rest of the 1946 Giants did, in fact, finish dead last, 36 games out. The top end of the 1946 race featured a lot of the same names as those of 1941 and 1942, including Slaughter, Moore, Max Lanier, Pee Wee Reese, Dixie Walker, Pete Reiser, Billy Herman, Kirby Higbe, and Joe Medwick. Many of these men, however, were returning after three or four seasons in the armed forces. They were older; they had not played much baseball; and they did not have a lot left. Herman, for example, was 36 years old; he would retire 15 games into the 1947 season. Medwick was 34 and Reiser was a very banged up 27; both were at or near the end as regular players. If St. Louis had any kind of youth movement, its name was Stan Musial. Still only 25 years old, the veteran outfielder-turned–first baseman batted .365 with 124 runs, 228 hits, 50 doubles, and 20 triples—all league-leading figures. The Dodgers, on the other hand, were beginning to rebuild in earnest under new boss Branch Rickey. A worshipper of youth, Rickey uttered the famous maxim: "It's better to get rid of a player a year too early than a year too late." Rickey's 1946 club already contained a few seeds of the great Brooklyn dynasty of the 1950s: the 29-year-old Eddie Stanky was ready to push Billy Herman aside at second; Reese, still only 27, played shortstop; 22-year-old Carl Furillo played right field; 22-year-old Bruce Edwards was the starting catcher; and the 20-year-old Ralph Branca and the 21-year-old Rex Barney pitched out of the bullpen. Playing second base for the Montreal Royals, the Dodgers's top farm club, was African-American second-base prospect Jackie Robinson.

The Cardinals, pre-season favorites, struggled unsuccessfully all season long to get away from the underdog Dodgers. Even the loss of the ill-fated Pete Reiser, who fractured his ankle in a pickoff play against Philadelphia, did not slow the Dodgers down. St. Louis dropped as far as 7½ games back on July 2, but then, after a slow fade that foreshadowed the collapse of 1951, the Dodgers backed into a season-ending tie with the Cardinals to necessitate the first pennant playoff. A never-before-used NL rule required that the two clubs play a best two-out-of-three series. Dodgers manager Leo Durocher won the coin toss and chose to play game one in St. Louis, thereby guaranteeing his team the home-field advantage in games two and three, but his strategy backfired as young lefty Howie Pollett threw a complete-game 4-2 victory over Ralph Branca. The two clubs then traveled to Brooklyn, where Lefty Joe Hatten pitched for the home team and righty Murry Dickson countered for the visitors. Hatten was shelled and Brooklyn went into the ninth inning trailing by a score of 8-1. Suddenly, the Dodgers gave their fans hope by staging a three-run rally and then loading the bases with one out. But the normally reliable Stanky struck out against veteran left-hander Harry Brecheen, as did right-handed pinch-hitter Howie Schultz, and the Cardinals were NL champions.

CHAPTER SIX

Monopoly Border War: The Mexican Invasion and the Gardella Case

The period from 1916 through World War II was a historic low point in players' rights, salaries, and influence over the game. The reason for this is simple. After the 1915 collapse of the Federal League, a rival major league that operated outside of organized baseball, the major leagues were left free to operate as an unchallenged—and legal—monopoly, arbitrarily setting whatever salaries and working conditions they pleased. Throughout the 1920s and 1930s, players remained bound by the reserve clause. Invented by NL founder William Hulbert in the late 1870s, the reserve clause was a standard part of every major-league player contract. The reserve clause kept players bound to one team indefinitely by giving teams the option to renew players' expired contracts at their old salary; players, on the other hand, could be released on ten days' notice if their employers no longer needed them. Many received poor medical care and played under nonguaranteed contracts, meaning that they received nothing if they got hurt and found themselves unable to play. Apart from a few superstars, they were severely underpaid and forced to pay out of their own pockets for such petty items as hats, uniforms, and spring-training living expenses. The vast majority of players arrived in spring training thoroughly out of baseball shape because they were forced to work at off-season non-baseball jobs in order to make ends meet. Since the 1910s, the players had had no union or organization of any kind to represent their interests. The attitude of organized baseball was that if players did not like their working conditions or their one-sided contracts, they could find another job—in another profession.

Things began to change in 1946, the year thousands of former professional players returned home from the war. A new federal law called the Veterans Act required that all returning servicemen be guaranteed their old jobs back for one year and be paid no less than their previous salary. The baseball owners refused to obey this law. When Philadelphia Phillies first baseman Tony Lupien came home to find himself sold to the Pacific Coast League (PCL) Hollywood Stars, he appealed to commissioner Chandler. It is hard to imagine former commissioner Kenesaw Mountain Landis not reacting with outrage to the Phillies' treatment of a returning vet and ordering Lupien's immediate reinstatement. Sadly, Chandler was no Landis; Lupien got back his registered letter, unopened, from the commissioner's office. His only choice was to bring his case to the Selective Service Board in Pennsylvania.

Frightened of losing the Lupien case, the Phillies offered the first baseman a deal: if he dropped the case he could play for Hollywood at his former major-league salary of $8,000 per year; advised by his lawyer that organized baseball could drag his case through the courts for years, Lupien agreed. Soon, a minor leaguer named Al Nimiec brought another similar case against the PCL Seattle Rainiers. This time the dispute went to federal court, where Judge Lloyd Black of the Western

District of Washington State ruled strongly in the player's favor. "Youth must be served," Black wrote, "but not at the expense of men who have worn the uniform and contrary to law." Like many previous judges, Black went on to condemn baseball's standard player contract as "reminiscent of chattels [slavery]" and to wonder aloud about the constitutionality of baseball's antitrust exemption. A by-product of various legal battles that came out of the economic war between organized baseball and the Federal League in the 1910s, the antitrust exemption was the main reason that organized baseball was allowed to operate as an unregulated monopoly—fixing prices, colluding on contracts, and discouraging competition by strictly controlling who could own or operate major- and minor-league teams. Baseball's exemption from antitrust laws was unique in all of U.S. business. If, for instance, a number of automobile companies got together to form a cartel, or monopoly, and fixed car prices, divided up the nation into separate markets belonging to only one company, and agreed to pay their workers the same or similar salaries, using the same standard contract—and blackballed any outside or dissenting company or worker from the entire industry—the federal government would step in and bring an antitrust lawsuit and the courts would break up the cartel. Even though modern players have come a long way—they now have a union, far better working conditions, and are paid much higher salaries—organized baseball's antitrust exemption survives in a limited form today.

The case of Al Nimiec was unusual. Hundreds of other players who returned from serving their country only to find themselves demoted or discarded by their former baseball employers simply accepted their treatment. Ultimately, however, the accumulated bad feeling caused by baseball's unfairness toward returning veterans combined with other factors to create momentum for change. One of those other factors was an effort by a labor organizer named Robert Murphy to form a major-league baseball players' union to fight for players' rights; the other was an attack on the major-league monopoly from south of the border in the person of a fabulously wealthy Mexican businessman named Jorge Pasquel. Pasquel controlled the Mexican League, a professional league that operated outside of organized baseball and, therefore, was not bound by the rules of the U.S. baseball monopoly, including the reserve clause. In the spring of 1946, Pasquel and a team of recruiters made the rounds of major-league spring training camps, offering big-league players huge contracts to play in Mexico. Meanwhile, Murphy formed the American Baseball Guild, announced that the guild would try to negotiate, among other things, a minimum wage for major-league players, impartial arbitration of disputes between employee and employer, and elimination of the infamous ten days' clause.

Anyone who remembered the baseball monopoly wars of the late nineteenth and early twentieth century could see a familiar pattern developing. The more the organized baseball monopoly succeeded, the more inflated the value of its franchises became, the more its labor costs decreased, and the more angry and oppressed the players felt. Angry players form labor unions. The combination of high profits for club owners and low salaries for players proved very tempting to would-be investors from outside the monopoly. If all you had to do to own a baseball club was to rent a ballpark and hire 25 players at a tiny fraction of what you would bring in through ticket sales, then the only obstacle to raking in huge profits was the baseball monopoly itself; and the answer to that problem was to gather a few like-minded investors, form another league, and offer major-league players big raises to jump to your league. As the Nimiec case and many others had demonstrated, the courts were very unlikely to stop you by upholding the reserve clause. The formation of rival leagues had always had two effects: one, it gave the players and their union leverage to play off one league against another to improve working conditions; and two, it vividly demonstrated to the players what their real value was on the open market. As in the nineteenth century, it was an eye-opening experience for a player making $5,000 per year to discover that another club was offering $20,000 for his services.

The men who ran organized baseball were blind to what history had been trying to show them for three quarters of a century: by paying their players bottom dollar, they were, in effect, devaluing their most important asset and both asking for labor trouble and encouraging outside attacks on their tightly-controlled, highly profitable monopoly. A typical reaction to the events of 1946 was that of Washington Senators owner Clark Griffith, who shouted that the sky was about to fall. "If the reserve clause is killed," Griffith cried, "there won't be any big leagues or little leagues." In their 1980 book *The Imperfect Diamond,* a classic study of baseball's labor history, authors Lee Lowenfish and Tony Lupien (yes, the same Tony Lupien who fought the Phillies over the Veterans Act in 1946) point out the irony of Griffith's words:

> *Griffith of course had been Ban Johnson's most avid recruiter of National Leaguers when the American League was fighting to get established. That was ancient history now. Since he had become a full owner in Washington in 1920, Griffith had been able to prosper personally and keep many of his family on the payroll while running a chronically noncontending franchise. He had maintained a team using many Latin American ballplayers whom he paid very little. Some observers thought there was poetic justice in the Mexican League raids,*

given Griffith's past practices, which had drawn a rebuke from Commissioner Landis in 1943 after rising complaints from Latin American baseball officials.[1]

Pasquel had mixed success in his efforts to hire major-league stars. Yankees shortstop Phil Rizzuto turned down a large raise to leave New York. St. Louis Cardinals star Stan Musial met with Pasquel in his hotel room and watched the Mexican League magnate lay $50,000 in certified checks on the bed. Musial also said no, preferring to remain with the Cardinals at $13,000 per year. Ted Williams turned down a mind-boggling $500,000 over three years; the Red Sox were paying him $40,000. Several lesser stars did take Pasquel's money, among them Dodgers catcher Mickey Owen, Cardinals pitcher Max Lanier, slugging Browns short-stop Vern Stephens, Giants pitcher Sal "The Barber" Maglie (so-called because he liked to "shave" hitters with fastballs up and in), Dodgers outfielder Luis Olmo, and Giants outfielder Danny Gardella. Commissioner Chandler's reaction was to announce that any player who did not return to his major-league club before the end of spring training, 1946, would be banned from organized baseball for five years. Pasquel scoffed at the ban and jokingly offered Chandler a hefty raise to become commissioner of the Mexican League.

Eventually, the Mexican League threat petered out; fear of being blackballed and word out of Mexico of poor playing conditions persuaded most major leaguers to stay put. Most of the jumpers quickly backed out of their Mexican League contracts and returned to the United States. Murphy, meanwhile, made a stand for his players guild in Pittsburgh, a strongly pro-union city where the players' guild had 90 percent support among the Pirates players. Rebuffed in his attempts to force the team to recognize the guild as the legal representative

On June 7, 1946, Robert Murphy, head of the American Baseball Guild, knocks on the Pirates locker-room door while the team's players hold a strike vote. The vote fell one short of the two-thirds majority required for a strike.

of its players, Murphy and the Pirates scheduled a strike vote for June 7. As the time for the vote approached, Murphy was optimistic; 48-year-old Pittsburgh manager Frankie Frisch prepared a line-up that included both himself and the 72-year-old Honus Wagner, then a Pirates coach. Fifteen thousand fans waited in the stands at Forbes Field, some wondering if they were going to see a game at all, others, perhaps, wondering if current Hall of Famer Wagner still had it at shortstop. At the last minute, however, the players blinked. Fearful of losing their careers and swayed by personal appeals from popular owner Bill Benswanger and promanagement teammates Rip Sewell and Jimmy Brown, the vote fell short of the two-thirds majority required for a strike. As word of the vote spread and the team took the field, Sewell and Brown were booed.

THE YEAR: 1946

Coming off four years of military service, Red Sox slugger Ted Williams started the 1946 season on fire as the Red Sox built up an insurmountable lead over rival Detroit in the AL pennant race. Even though Williams's final stats look very good—.342 average, 38 home runs, and 123 RBIs—the Red Sox MVP did most of his damage early. Cleveland manager Lou Boudreau may have started Williams's second-half slump by implementing the infamous "Ted Williams overshift" in the second game of a July 14 doubleheader. Williams had homered three times in the opener and when he came to bat in the second game, he faced a defensive alignment that put every non-pitcher on the right side of second base except the catcher and the left fielder, who played deep shortstop. Williams laughed so hard that he had to ask for time to regain his composure. The shift became less and less funny as the season wore on; other managers copied it, and Williams stopped hitting. Many AL teams who did not employ the shift simply pitched around Williams, as evidenced by his 156 walks, the fourth-highest single-season total ever. In the 1946 World Series, the Cardinals tried both strategies, and a frustrated Williams walked five times and batted a dismal

.200 with no extra-base hits; to Boston fans Williams was the goat in Boston's four-games-to-three series loss to St. Louis.

Washington's Mickey Vernon captured the AL batting title at .353, and Hank Greenberg led in homers with 44 and RBIs with 127. Tigers ace Hal Newhouser won his second straight ERA title at 1.94, and Bob Feller set a new single-season strikeout record with 348, breaking Rube Waddell's venerable 1904 mark.

The National League race was disrupted when several players from contending teams jumped to the Mexican League, which was offering underpaid U.S. major leaguers huge increases in salary. The pennant race was affected, as the Dodgers lost Mickey Owen and Luis Olmo, and the Cardinals lost left-handed starting pitcher Max Lanier, who had started the 1946 NL season 6–0 with a 1.93 ERA.

The NL race came down to a knock-down, drag-out fight between St. Louis and Brooklyn, two teams that shared many personnel, including GM Branch Rickey and the only brother combination to have won batting titles: Harry Walker of the Cardinals and Dixie Walker of Brooklyn. NL MVP Stan Musial and Enos Slaughter were the twin engines that powered the Cardinals attack; Musial batted a league-leading .365 and also led in runs with 124, doubles with 50 and triples with 20, and the .300-hitting Slaughter scored 100 runs and drove in a league-high 130. With Lanier gone, Howie Pollet became the ace of the St. Louis staff, going 21–10 with an NL-leading 2.10 ERA; Murry Dickson and Harry Brecheen each won 15 games. The Dodgers were led by Pete Reiser, who stole a league-leading 34 bases; Dixie Walker, who had 116 RBIs and second baseman Eddie Stanky, who drew 137 walks to lead the NL in on-base average at .436. St. Louis won the play-off, 2–0, on Pollet's 4-2 complete-game defeat of Ralph Branca and an 8-1 drubbing in game two.

Stan Musial checks out his lumber before a September 14, 1946 game. Musial won the NL MVP that year, and his Cardinals won the World Series over the Boston Red Sox.

The Cardinals won the World Series in seven well-pitched games. As has happened so many times in post-season history, and for whatever the reason, the big guys in the 1946 World Series bombed—Musial hit .222 and Williams hit .200—vacating center stage in favor of little guys like Rudy York, Harry Brecheen, and Country Slaughter. Even rookie catcher Joe Garagiola had a four-hit game. Ex-Tiger York's tenth-inning homer won game one for the Red Sox, and the teams exchanged victories until the final game. With the score 3-3 in the top of the eighth, the still-slumping Ted Williams popped up to leave the go-ahead run on second. Then in the bottom half, Slaughter singled and scored the winning run on a two-out single to left-center off the bat of Harry Walker. Some observers felt that Red Sox shortstop Johnny Pesky was taken by surprise on the play and hesitated an instant before relaying the throw from the outfield to the plate.

This play is still being debated today; it was even reenacted, with many of the original participants, at a recent old-timer's game. Did Pesky hesitate before relaying the centerfielder's throw home? Was it second baseman Doerr's or third baseman Higgins's fault for not warning Pesky where the runner was? Or did Boston do everything more or less right, but Slaughter, with two outs and the World Series winner's share on the line, simply ran three base-lengths faster than two men could throw a baseball roughly the same distance?

In spite of Murphy's failure in Pittsburgh, the major-league owners were much more afraid of Murphy and unionization than they were of Pasquel and his Mexican League. During the 1946 season the owners adopted a strategy of coopting the union movement. Carefully controlled meetings were held at which player representatives aired their grievances. In July, the owners announced a series of reforms, which included a minimum major-league salary of $5,500, a maximum annual pay cut of 25 percent, a meager pension plan for retired ballplayers, and a requirement that clubs pay players' living expenses during spring training. Until recently, this was still referred to in big-league lingo as

"Murphy Money." The program did not include any change in the reserve clause, although the ten days clause was extended to 30 days. The owners' new strategy worked. Players were satisfied with the reforms offered them and feared losing their careers if they pushed too hard on an independent union. By the end of the 1946 season Murphy and his guild were history. Accusing the owners of creating what amounted to a company union, a bitter Robert Murphy retired from the scene, but not before he uttered these prophetic words: "The players have been offered an apple, but they could have had an orchard."

No longer worried about Robert Murphy or Jorge Pasquel, the major-league owners dealt harshly with the Mexican League jumpers. Commissioner Chandler announced that baseball intended to enforce a five-year ban on players under contract who had gone to Mexico and a three-year ban on those who had violated the reserve clause. The troubles of 1946, however, did not disappear quite as easily as that. One of the banned players, ex-Giant Danny Gardella, hired a lawyer and took organized baseball to court. Gardella was one of the few major leaguers who enjoyed playing in Mexico; after playing out the season, however, he decided to return and found himself, along with catcher Mickey Owen and pitcher Max Lanier, banned from organized baseball. He played in Cuba and on a barnstorming outfit called the Max Lanier All-Stars. Lanier's team suffered from a shortage of willing opponents because Chandler announced that the ban would also be enforced against any minor leaguer, major leaguer, or Negro Leaguer who took the field with or against a banned player. By 1947 Gardella was out of baseball completely and working for $36 a week as an orderly in a New York hospital. His only crime had been to play out his Giants contract and then honor his Mexican League contract while reserved by the Giants. He met with a lawyer named Frederic Johnson, who studied the matter and urged Gardella to sue on the basis that the reserve clause violated federal antitrust laws. Johnson pointed out that the reserve clause had never been upheld in a court of law and that, since the Federal League War, baseball had never even attempted to argue the legality of the reserve clause. Only in baseball, where autocratic owners bullied powerless, unsophisticated players, would the idea even be taken seriously that by signing a single one-year contract, a person was permanently signing away his right to negotiate another deal when the first contract expired. Yet this is what the reserve clause amounted to; if a rookie signed a one-year contract for $10,000 per year, when the contract was up the team had the option of renewing the contract at a lower salary (no more than 25 percent lower after 1946) each year *ad infinitum.* The player had no way of escaping his obligation to the team or any bargaining power to negotiate a raise, no matter how well he performed, other than threatening to retire, in which case no other club in organized baseball would employ him. If, on the other hand, the team had no further use for the player, it could release him at any time without obligation. Anywhere in America outside of a baseball park, the concept of the reserve clause would be considered laughable.

Gardella's case proceeded through the courts, and a trial was scheduled for November 1949. Organized baseball was shaking in its boots; an overheated Branch Rickey accused opponents of the reserve clause of "Communistic tendencies." Commissioner Chandler, however, tried to head off further lawsuits by issuing an amnesty and reinstating Owen, Maglie, Lanier, and the rest of the banned players. The Gardella case, however, never went to trial. Pressure for compromise was building on both sides, on Gardella because he was getting older and rustier, and on baseball from its own lawyers, who painted a grim—and expensive—scenario of massive player free agency should they lose the Gardella case. Gardella settled for $60,000 in cash and a contract with the St. Louis Cardinals for 1950. (His major-league career lasted one more at bat; after flying out his first time up with St. Louis, Gardella was sent to the minors for good.) Speaking for his employers, Commissioner Chandler announced: "I feel so relieved. If I were a drinking man I'd get drunk." The bottom line on the labor troubles of 1946 was that organized baseball had won the early battles, including preserving its precious reserve clause, but these would turn out to be only the opening skirmishes in a long, bitter war over the major-league monopoly. Previous monopoly wars were, with the exception of the Players League war of 1890, fought between groups of rival owners. The war that began in 1946 was different; it matched the major-league baseball owners against their employees, the major-league players. It is too soon to say who won and who lost. The war begun by Robert Murphy and Danny Gardella is still being fought today.

$\mathcal{S}$ubway Series:
The Yankees Versus
the Dodgers

The frenzied excitement leading up to the World Series
of 1941 was like nothing New York City had ever seen.
Not that a subway, or all–New York, series was anything new; five times in the past, most recently in 1937,
the New York Giants had met the New York Yankees in
October. The difference this time was that Brooklyn was
involved; for the first time, a subway series crossed the
East River. The rivalry between the former sister cities—
now united politically, if not spiritually, as the New York
City boroughs of Manhattan and Brooklyn—dated back to
the old amateur days of baseball in the 1850s, when the
best players from each side of the river met at Flushing
Race Course for a series of all-star contests. It was there
that fans, for the first time, paid money to see a game
of baseball. In the twentieth century the Brooklyn–New
York rivalry had taken on a new shape, as ex-Giant
catcher Wilbert "Uncle Robbie" Robinson's perennially
noncontending Brooklyn Dodgers brought up the
rear of the National League while John McGraw's
Giants dynasty won pennant after pennant. The toast of

Broadway and the glitzy Manhattan social scene, the New York Giants were the Yankees of the pre–World War II era. The Dodgers, on the other hand, were the Daffiness Boys or, simply, Dem Bums, a collection of odd characters prone to bizarre miscues and breath-taking collapses that seemed somehow to fit Brooklyn's image as the home of the downtrodden, the unwashed, and the eccentric. While Manhattan fans boasted of classy winners like Christy Mathewson, Rube Marquard, Mel Ott, Bill Terry, and Carl Hubbell, Brooklynites rooted no less passionately for flawed stars like the taci-turn Zach Wheat, the crowd-pleasing Dazzy Vance, the naturally comic Casey Stengel, and the just plain goofy Babe Herman. One of the few positive memories of those times from a Brooklyn point of view was the race of 1934, when an off-the-cuff preseason remark by Giants manager Bill Terry—"Is Brooklyn still in the league?"—inspired the last-place Dodgers to rise up and knock their cross-river rivals out of the pennant race in a dramatic, late-season upset.

Now the Giants were down, but like a restless lover Manhattan had already abandoned the older New York team for an even more glamorous newcomer, the New York Yankees of Babe Ruth and Lou Gehrig. The Yankees had lost some of their luster with the passing of those two in the late 1930s, but in 1941 the team seemed to be building a new dynasty around the growing legend of centerfielder Joe DiMaggio. Under an innovative and new team president, Larry MacPhail, the Brooklyn Dodgers were beginning to build a real winner for the first time. A good friend of Branch Rickey, the heavy-drinking, loud-mouthed MacPhail had Rickey's unerr-ing eye for talent without his sense of moderation. As Leo Durocher once said, "They say there is a fine line between genius and insanity, and MacPhail is con-stantly wandering over the line." MacPhail rebuilt the Dodgers by bringing in veteran infielder Billy Herman, pitcher Kirby Higbe, outfielder Joe Medwick, and catcher Mickey Owen in trades. He bought slugging first baseman Dolph Camilli, pitcher Whitlow Wyatt, outfielder Dixie Walker, and promising prospect Pete Reiser. He brought up relief ace Hugh Casey from the minors. In 1937 the team had traded for ex–Gas House Gang shortstop Durocher, who was not getting along with St. Louis manager Frankie Frisch, and in 1939 MacPhail made Durocher player/manager. Durocher and MacPhail were one of baseball's all-time fun couples—the Billy Martin and George Steinbrenner of the 1940s. When he was not himself resigning in a drunken huff, the Dodgers president was quarreling with Durocher or firing him in a rage. The first time it happened, Durocher was solemnly packing his bags the next morning when a hung-over and soft-spoken MacPhail telephoned him to discuss a possible trade; the previous night's firing was never mentioned again. After that, Durocher and the Brooklyn press corps learned to double-check the next day before assuming that Durocher had really been let go.

The 1941 race ended with Durocher being fired once again, this time for ordering the Dodgers victory train to bypass New York's 125th Street station on the way home from the pennant-clinching game in Boston. Durocher was afraid that after three hours of uninhibited celebration some of his drunken players might exit the train at the wrong stop; what he did not know was that MacPhail had been waiting to board the train and join the party at 125th Street. As usual, Durocher was rehired the following morning. The train was met at Grand Central station in mid-Manhattan by a crowd of more than ten thousand Brooklyn fans carrying signs that read: "The Bums Done It" and "Are the Giants Still in the League?" Yankee fans were, of course, excited about the upcoming subway series—and confident; with a star-studded lineup that included DiMaggio, Rizzuto, Henrich, Keller, Dickey, Gordon, and Rolfe,

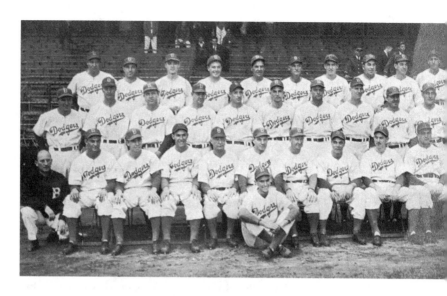

*The 1941 Brooklyn Dodgers pose for a team photo.
Affectionately known by their fans as Dem Bums,
the Dodgers overcame years of mediocrity and
frustration to take the National League pennant.*

the team was coming off a streak of nine straight post-season wins going back to 1937. Lefty Gomez was ill, but the Yankees still had a solid pitching staff of Red Ruffing, Marius Russo, Spud Chandler, and Johnny Murphy. Nothing, however, could match the joy felt in Brooklyn. The borough threw a nonstop party that lasted for days, culminating with the Dodgers players riding in a motorcade from the Grand Army Plaza near Prospect Park down Flatbush Avenue and Fulton Street to what was now Borough Hall and what had once been Brooklyn's City Hall. An estimated one million fans lined the motorcade route. Some came dressed in bum costumes; others were there to urge the team to, as one sign written in Brooklynese—the inimitable Brooklyn dialect—put it, "Moideh Duh Yanks."

With the first two games of the 1941 World Series scheduled for Yankee Stadium, Durocher held back his two aces, Higbe and Wyatt, and pitched second-line starter Curt Davis in the opener against Yankees ace Red Ruffing. Durocher's surprise tactic almost paid off, but the Dodgers lost, 3-2. Brooklyn squandered a pair of late-inning opportunities, one when pinch-hitter Jimmy Wasdell hit a foul pop-up with men on first and second and none out in the seventh. Durocher later claimed that Wasdell had missed a bunt sign. To make matters worse, shortstop Pee Wee Reese tried to tag up and advance to third base on the play, but was tagged out by an alert Phil Rizzuto. Brooklyn evened up the series the next day with a 3-2 win by Wyatt. Meanwhile, the closeness of the two contests was causing growing tension on the field. Several times base runners leveled shortstops Rizzuto and Reese while they were attempting to turn double plays. After Mickey Owen slid with his spikes up into the Yankee shortstop in the fifth inning of game two, the New Yorkers threatened to retaliate. "They're gonna get some of that rough stuff, too," second baseman Joe Gordon told reporters after the game, "and you can put that in the paper." The Dodgers responded to Gordon's threat with a collective shrug. "I ain't going nowhere," Owen said, to which Durocher added: "They want to play rough? Well, that suits us. That's when we play our best ball."

The first game in Brooklyn matched right-handed Dodgers knuckleballer Freddie Fitzsimmons against Yankees lefty Marius Russo. The Dodgers' home ballpark, Ebbets Field, had a special atmosphere that no other park could match. Millions of fans listened to the 1941 series on the radio, enjoying the play-by-play of legendary broadcasters Red Barber and Mel Allen, but to really appreciate the Brooklyn Dodgers, you had to be there in person. Built by team owner Charles Ebbets in the 1910s, an era when five thousand fans was a big crowd, Ebbets Field was remarkably small and intimate. The fences were short and asymmetrical, which encouraged run-scoring; to further aid hitters and spectators foul territory was kept to a minimum. Supported by pillars, not cantilevered like most modern parks, the upper deck hung directly over the foul lines, bringing the fans so close to the action that the ballplayers not only did not pretend, like their modern counterparts, to ignore their presence, but also frequently knew individual fans by name. Brooklynites exchanged comments and banter with the Dodgers in the field; some fans, like Hilda Chester and her cowbell, became famous for their trademark cheers or eccentric rooting style. This intimacy produced a unique feeling of community between fans and players. Calling themselves the Dodger Symphony, five particularly rabid fans roamed the Ebbets Field stands playing ragtime music and letting loose an embarrassing cymbal crash when, after an out, an opposing player's rear end made contact with the bench. The umpires had to put up with the organist playing "Three Blind Mice" (NL umpiring crews then consisted of three men, not four as they do today) whenever they ran out onto the field to start a game. Needless to say, the Dodgers enjoyed a tremendous home-field advantage.

For six innings of game three Russo and Fitzsimmons held the hitters scoreless; then in the top of the seventh Russo hit a low line drive that struck Fitzsimmons squarely on the knee and ricocheted on the fly to shortstop Pee Wee Reese. Reese grabbed the ball for an out, but Fitzsimmons collapsed in pain. He was carried off the field with a fractured kneecap. Hugh Casey then came in to pitch. An alcoholic loner who later shot himself to death in a suicide resembling that of his drinking buddy, writer Ernest Hemingway, Casey was a typical 1941 Dodger—mean, aggressive, and ready to fight at the drop of a hat. Perhaps disconcerted by

Fitzsimmons's injury, Casey promptly allowed two runs, and Brooklyn lost, 2-1. Up in the press box, an irrational Larry MacPhail ranted and blamed Durocher for the loss, saying that Casey had not been adequately warmed up.

Down two games to one with only two remaining home games, the Dodgers were desperate to win game four. Unfortunately, 22-game-winner Higbe did not have it and was knocked out of the game early, after allowing three runs in 3⅔ innings. But the Dodgers got to New York starter Atley Donald and led 4-3 after Reiser's two-run homer in the fifth. Reliever Hugh Casey, the goat of game three, then bore down and pitched brilliantly. The Dodgers' bats went silent, but Casey breezed through the late innings. The off-balance Yankees sluggers launched one easy pop fly after another. In the top of the ninth, Casey got first baseman Johnny Sturm to ground out to second. Third baseman Rolfe tapped weakly back to the mound for out number two. All Casey had to do was retire Tommy Henrich and the series would be tied two games apiece with three games to go. The count went to one ball and two strikes. Catcher Mickey Owen called for a curveball— although some observers later swore that it was actually a spitball—and Casey wound up and fired. Henrich later told what happened next: "It looked like a fastball. Then when it broke, it broke so sharply that it was out of the strike zone. So I tried to hold up, but I wasn't able to." The umpire called strike three. The Brooklyn crowd cheered and some jumped onto the field and began to celebrate, but suddenly they fell silent. Owen had missed the ball, which was rolling toward the fence behind him. Henrich took off and reached first base safely.

There was a saying about the old Yankees that if you opened the door for them even a crack, they would knock it down and beat you. That aptly describes what happened next. DiMaggio slashed a hard single to left.

The Dodgers and the Yankees appear equally matched on the cover of the 1941 World Series program. This series tilted the Yankees way in the fourth game when a Dodgers error turned an apparent loss into victory.

With a count of 0-2, powerful Charlie Keller hit a double off the outfield wall that scored two runs; the Yankees now led, 5-4. Bill Dickey walked and Joe Gordon doubled in Keller and Dickey for two insurance runs. Yankees reliever Johnny Murphy set down the dazed Dodgers one, two, three in the bottom of the ninth, and the game was over. The series ended the next day, as New York's Ernie Bonham outdueled Whitlow Wyatt 3-1.

The Dodgers were emotionally crushed. Mickey Owen was in tears after the game; ripped by the press for not blocking Casey's strike-three pitch to Henrich, he became the World Series goat. Hugh Casey took defeat so hard that a worried Leo Durocher scrambled frantically to deflect the blame onto himself. Durocher told reporters that the loss was his fault for not going out to the mound to settle the rattled Casey down after he got two strikes on Keller. "For the first time in my life," Durocher confessed, "I was shell-shocked." The following day Brooklyn's daily newspaper, *The Brooklyn Eagle,* ran a headline that would become a catch phrase in Brooklyn through many years—and many more post-season disappointments—to come. It said: WAIT TILL NEXT YEAR.

CHAPTER
EIGHT

$\mathscr{B}$rown Dodgers: Robinson and Rickey Erase the Color Line Forever

During the war years, the military draft caused a severe labor shortage in many American industries. As in World War I, labor shortages forced U.S. industry to open up to women and African-Americans high-paying blue-collar jobs that had been held predominantly by white men. Color lines that had excluded African-Americans for decades fell in a number of industries. President Franklin Roosevelt pushed the process along by establishing the Federal Commission on Fair Employment Practices to combat racial discrimination. Unlike the case of World War I, however, the positive effects of World War II on the lives of many African-Americans and other minorities did not end abruptly with the cease-fire. There was no repeat of the bloody race riots of 1919 in 1946. On the contrary, African-Americans held onto many of the economic gains that they had made as the government continued the push for further racial reforms. New York State passed the Quinn-Ives Act in 1942, which prohibited racial discrimination in hiring, and in 1945 it established the

New York State Commission Against Discrimination, the first state agency of its kind in the country. In 1946 President Truman set up federal commissions on higher education and civil rights to try to remedy racial discrimination and segregation in those areas. That same year, the Navy began to experiment with racially mixed units; in 1948 Truman ordered the army to desegregate completely. In the aftermath of World War II, the nation took the first, tentative steps toward the Civil Rights movement that would transform U.S. society in the two decades to come.

Baseball experienced a wartime labor shortage, too; by 1943 enough of the top players had enlisted or been drafted that the quality of play in the majors suffered greatly. Still, the major-league owners refused to hire any of the hundreds of qualified African-American players in the Negro Leagues. Part of the reason was Kenesaw Mountain Landis, who throughout his long tenure as commissioner effectively used his power to cut short any debate on the issue of the color line. While he was in office, not only was the color line strictly observed, but he fined or reprimanded anyone in the game who even dared to talk publicly about the subject. In 1942, after Dodgers manager Leo Durocher was reported as saying that there were "about a million" Negro Leaguers who could play in the majors if it were not for the color line, Landis called him on the carpet of his Chicago office and convinced him that he had been misquoted. "There is no rule," Landis said, "formal or informal, or any understanding—unwritten, subterranean, or sub-anything—against the hiring of Negro players by the teams of Organized Baseball."

As early as the late 1920s and 1930s, however, cracks had begun to show in baseball's Jim Crow facade. Part of the reason had to do with international politics. By the mid-1930s, it was becoming more and more obvious that the rise of Adolf Hitler and the racist Nazi party in

Germany was a potential threat to the United States. Most Americans were repelled by Nazism and over-joyed when African-American sprinter Jesse Owens embarrassed the Germans by winning several gold medals. Besides making an African-American athlete a national hero in the United States, the Nazis' vile racist and anti-Semitic politics also had the effect of discredit-ing white supremacism at home. Organized baseball became increasingly defensive about its segregationist policies. Newspaper columnist Westbrook Pegler fired the opening shot in a media attack on the baseball color line that would intensify as the 1930s went on. He ridiculed the baseball owners as hypocrites. "The magnates," he wrote, "haven't the gall to put [the color line] on paper." In 1933 sportswriter Jimmy Powers polled baseball managers and executives and discov-ered that nearly all of them favored integrating baseball. African-American reporters like Wendell Smith of the *Pittsburgh Courier,* the country's most prestigious African-American paper, kept up the pressure. In 1945, after Red Sox general manager Eddie Collins said that his team had never considered hiring an African-American player because none had ever asked for a tryout, Smith showed up in Boston with Jackie Robinson and two other Negro Leaguers. The Red Sox were forced to hold the tryout, although it would be 14 years before the team would sign its first African-American player, infielder Elijah "Pumpsie" Green. In response to criticism from the press, NL President John Heydler repeated the party line that denied the existence of a color line. "I do not recall one instance," he said, "where baseball has allowed either race, creed, or color to enter into its selection of players." During the war, it became harder and harder to say words like these with a straight face. With American soldiers of both races fighting and dying to defeat the Nazis, racial segregation never looked more wrong to white America. The Jim Crow policy of baseball—an institution that enjoyed an exemption from wartime restrictions based on its status as a patriotic institution—seemed particularly obscene.

Even before the end of World War II it was clear to many in baseball that integration was on the way. In 1938 Clark Griffith said that the end of segregation was "not far off." NL President Ford Frick said that "baseball is biding its time and waiting for the social change which is inevitable. Times are changing." Yet progress was excruciatingly slow. Even after the death of staunch segregationist Kenesaw Mountain Landis in 1944, organized baseball held fast to the color line. Landis's successor, Happy Chandler of Kentucky, gave African-Americans hope by telling the *Pittsburgh Courier* in an interview: "If [African-Americans] can fight and die on Okinawa, Guadalcanal, in the South Pacific, they can play ball in America." But nothing changed until 1946, when the color line was suddenly rocked to its foundations. That was when Brooklyn Dodgers president Branch Rickey signed Kansas City Monarchs infielder Jackie Robinson to play for Brooklyn's top farm club, the International League (IL) Montreal Royals. Rickey made no secret of his intention to promote Robinson to the majors as soon as he was ready. In response, the major-league owners met in secret to vote on the question of whether to allow African-Americans into the majors. The result of the vote was 15-1 against. Brooklyn Dodgers president Branch Rickey cast the only ballot in favor, but otherwise took no notice of the vote. Baseball commissioner Happy Chandler spent much of his later life campaigning for some of the credit for Rickey's breaking of the baseball color line. He claimed that he and Rickey were secretly working together all along and that Rickey even asked him for permission to go ahead with the signing of Robinson. "I have never understood," said Chandler years later, "why Branch Rickey took the full credit for breaking the color line with Jackie Robinson. If I hadn't approved the contract transfer from Montreal, the Dodgers farm, to Brooklyn, Robinson couldn't have played. No chance." There is little reason, however, to look upon this as anything more than pure hot air. If Chandler had not approved Robinson's contract transfer from Montreal, he probably would have opened up organized baseball to a devastating lawsuit or civil rights prosecution. In all probability, Chandler did nothing in 1946 because he did not know what to do and the owners did not know what to tell him to do. Other than Chandler's own word, there is no evidence that he took any action against the color line or gave Rickey or Robinson any help at all.

On, April 18, 1946, Opening Day of the IL season, second baseman Jackie Robinson stepped up to the plate wearing the blue and white Montreal uniform. The first African-American to play in organized baseball in almost 50 years and the first to play in the IL since the days of Bud Fowler, George Stovey, Fleet Walker, and Frank Grant back in the nineteenth century, Robinson went four for five with two stolen bases as the Royals destroyed the Jersey City Giants 14-1. As Branch Rickey would tell the story years later, this was the culmination of years of careful planning and waiting for the right moment to break the baseball color line.

Wesley Branch Rickey (Rickey went by his middle name) was born in Ohio in 1881 into a strict Methodist family. Rickey was a good athlete who played and coached college baseball. When he became a professional baseball player in 1903, he promised his religious mother that he would never play on Sundays. That and an arm injury limited his major-league career to 119 games with the Browns and the Yankees. After his playing days were over Rickey left baseball to study law but soon decided that he preferred a career in sports. After managing the AL St. Louis Browns in the mid-1910s, he moved across town in 1919 to serve as president and manager of the NL Cardinals. It soon became clear that Rickey's talents lay in scouting and player development rather than on-field managing. Cardinals owner Sam Breadon hired superstar second baseman Rogers Hornsby to manage the team and put Rickey in charge of the front office. A genius at finding and evaluating baseball talent, Rickey turned the Cardinals into one of the all-time great NL dynasties. On the principle of "quality out of quantity" he built the first farm system. By the late 1930s, Rickey and the Cardinals had achieved control of 32 minor-league teams and over 600 players and had turned them into a massive baseball talent factory. Rickey hired the best instructors, scouts, and coaches and pioneered the use of batting cages, pitching machines, batting helmets, and efficient practice drills. For the next 25 years, this system provided a steady stream of talent that kept the Cardinals in contention almost every year and helped them win eight pennants. Rickey's system produced hard-nosed ballplayers like Dizzy Dean, Joe Medwick, and Pepper Martin of the colorful "Gas House Gang" team of 1934. Just as important to a small-market team like St. Louis, it also provided plenty of players to trade and sell to other teams for cash. At one time 65 products of the Cardinals farm system were playing in the eight-team National League.

After a falling out with Breadon, Rickey moved to Brooklyn in 1942 to run the Dodgers. According to Rickey, that is when he began in secret to plot the breaking of the baseball color line. What was his motivation? Rickey's answer to that question was to tell the story of an ugly racial incident from his early college coaching days at Ohio Wesleyan University that had left a lasting mark on him. In 1904 the team traveled to South Bend, Indiana, to play Notre Dame; one member of the team was an African-American named Charley Thomas. When they arrived at their hotel, however, Rickey's players were told that African-Americans were not welcome. By threatening to move the team elsewhere, Rickey convinced the hotel to allow Thomas to stay on a cot in Rickey's room. Later that evening, Rickey entered his room to find Thomas sitting on the edge of the bed in tears, rubbing his hands together. "It's my skin, Mr. Rickey," Thomas cried, "If I could just make it go away I'd be like everybody else." Branch Rickey claimed that he never forgot that scene and that he had spent most of his 60 years in baseball waiting for the chance to do something about it.

That chance came when Rickey came to Brooklyn. According to Arthur Mann, Rickey's friend and biographer, while reporting to the Dodgers board of directors on his plan to set up a mass scouting system, Rickey mentioned mysteriously that he "might include a Negro player or two." That was in 1942, his first year with the Dodgers. Three years later Rickey announced to the public that he intended to establish a new Negro League called the United States League (USL). The plan called for a Brooklyn franchise named the Brooklyn Brown Dodgers that would play in the Dodgers ballpark, Ebbets Field; the USL would compete with the established, mostly African-American–owned Negro Leagues that fielded teams in both Yankee Stadium in the Bronx and the Polo Grounds in upper Manhattan and—to Rickey's annoyance—paid rent to the Dodgers' competitors. Some day, Rickey told reporters, the USL might be merged into organized baseball; the USL, however, never got off the ground and the Brown Dodgers folded after less than one year. Rickey later explained that the whole thing had been a smoke screen. The USL's real purpose, he said, was to provide a cover so that Rickey could send his Dodger scouts on a nationwide search for the right African-American player to break the color line without arousing the suspicion of the other baseball owners. The search continued through 1944 and 1945. Rickey felt that the twentieth century's first African-American player had to be a special kind of person. Mindful of the abuse that Fowler, Grant, and the others had taken from some white fans and players in the IL during the 1880s, Rickey feared that if he picked a man who was too sensitive or had too short a temper, the result would be ugly racial confrontations on the field or in the stands and that this would give racist owners the perfect justification for maintaining the color line. "I had to get a man," Rickey said, "who would carry the badge of martyrdom. The press had to accept him. He had to stimulate a good reaction to the Negro race itself for an unfortunate one might have solidified the antagonism of other colors. And I had to consider the man's teammates."

What he meant by that was that the player had to be acceptable to whites. Clyde Sukeforth was the Dodger scout chiefly in charge of the search for the right man. In August 1945 Rickey told Sukeforth to concentrate his efforts on Jackie Robinson. A rookie shortstop with the Kansas City Monarchs, a famous Negro League team whose big drawing card was aging superstar pitcher Satchel Paige, Robinson was unproven as a ballplayer, but he had other things going for him: he was sophisticated, well educated, and had already played competitive sports in an integrated setting. A graduate of the University of California at Los Angeles, Robinson had starred on the school's integrated football team. If he liked Robinson's potential as a baseball player, Sukeforth was to bring him to Brooklyn for a meeting with Rickey. When Sukeforth caught up with the Monarchs, Robinson was injured and could not play, but Sukeforth was very impressed with Robinson's personality. "There was something about that man that just gripped you," Sukeforth later remembered, "He was tough, he was intelligent and he was proud." Although Robinson was suspicious of Sukeforth and Rickey, he agreed to come to the Dodgers offices at 215 Montague Street in Brooklyn Heights and hear Rickey out.

Alone with Robinson, Rickey explained that he wanted to break the baseball color line by signing him to a Montreal contract; if things went well in the IL, then Robinson would be promoted to the Dodgers. The eloquent Rickey delivered a passionate sermon on the terrible verbal abuse, beanballs, and spikings that Robinson would face and why he had to accept them without retaliation. "You will symbolize a crucial cause," Rickey said, "one incident, just one incident, can set it back twenty years." Even though he was so personally prudish that he never uttered a stronger curse than "Judas Priest," Rickey vividly acted out the vile insults Robinson would have to endure: "dirty black son of a bitch, nigger bastard, coon!" Robinson nearly jumped up and took a swing at Rickey. "Are you looking for a man who is afraid to fight back," he asked. "No," said Rickey, "I'm looking for a ballplayer with guts enough not to fight back." After considering the idea for a few minutes, Jackie Robinson promised to try to turn the other cheek.

Robinson's signing was met with anger and disbelief by the other baseball owners, but other than passing the meaningless resolution condemning the move at their 1946 owners meeting, no real action was taken. As Robinson rolled along in Montreal on his way to the IL batting title at .349—putting the lie to all the old racist arguments that African-Americans could not compete with whites in professional baseball—the defenders of the color line in baseball fell strangely silent. The people of Brooklyn largely welcomed Robinson, even if they seemed to be motivated more out of team loyalty than idealism. One Brooklyn fan from that era remembered

Jackie Robinson (left) shakes hands with Brooklyn Dodgers president Branch Rickey after signing a contract to play for the Dodgers top minor-league affiliate in 1946.

that Robinson became just one more bone of contention in the ancient blood feud between Dodgers and Giants fans:

> All some wise-guy Giant fan had to say was "Hey Mac, you got a nigger on first base," and we'd reply: "What's it your business, Mac? He's better than anybody you got on your team. So what if he's black? He plays for Brooklyn, don't he?"[1]

The Dodgers signed four more African-American players, including catcher Roy Campanella and pitcher Don Newcombe. Commissioner Happy Chandler had no comment on the signings. The other owners seemed to be waiting to see what Rickey was going to do next. One reason for this was fear of public opinion, which in the years just after the war seemed increasingly opposed to segregation; another was fear of prosecution under the new state and federal civil-rights laws. This second fear was very real. As far as the law was concerned, keeping a secret "gentleman's agreement" was one thing; openly taking a player's job away because of race was another.

Rickey spent the winter of 1946 and 1947 preparing the way for Robinson's arrival in the major leagues. He met quietly with clergymen and other leaders of the African-American community in Brooklyn to ask their help in toning down the enthusiasm of African-American fans. As offensive as this sounds today, Rickey was quite sincere. Afraid of a white backlash, Rickey urged them not to spoil Robinson's chances as African-American fans in Chicago had spoiled Charlie "Chief Tokohama" Grant's in 1901. When trouble came, however, it came not from fans of either race but from Rickey's own players. During spring training of 1947, several of Robinson's future teammates, including Dixie Walker, Eddie Stanky, and Carl Furillo, signed a secret petition stating that they would refuse to play with an African-American. When he heard about this, Dodgers manager Leo Durocher handled the situation brilliantly. He hauled the players, including the dazed petitioners, out of bed in the middle of the night and assembled them, in their pajamas and underwear, in the hotel kitchen. Durocher then gave a talk about his favorite color—green:

I hear some of you fellows don't want to play with Robinson and that you have a petition drawn up that you're going to sign. Well, boys, you know what you can do with that petition. You can wipe your ass with it. I'm the manager of this ballclub and I'm interested in one thing. Winning. I'll play an elephant if he can do the job, and to make room for him I'll send my own brother home. This fellow is a real great ballplayer. He's going to win pennants for us. He's going to put money in your pockets and money in mine.[2]

When Rickey arrived, he offered to trade fan favorite Walker and any other members of the group who wanted out. He was serious; Dixie Walker was eventually sent to Pittsburgh in a trade for Preacher Roe, Billy Cox, and Gene Mauch. Nothing more was heard about the petition, and Jackie Robinson opened the 1947 season as Brooklyn's starting first baseman.

Robinson did not find the National League to be a very friendly place. In Philadelphia, the Dodgers team hotel refused to give him a room. In the early part of the season, his teammates ranged from indifferent to outright hateful. Just as Rickey had predicted, opposing teams subjected him to a torrent of awful verbal abuse, spikings, and pitches aimed at his head. Robinson was hit by pitches nine times in 1947. He was angry, but he turned that anger outward and used it to win ball games. Brooklyn outfielder Edwin "Duke" Snider remembered one example of this in a game against the Chicago Cubs.

Sam Jones was pitching, and we were down by one run, and he was throwing hard and we weren't hitting him. Jackie came up, and he threw a close pitch, and Jackie started jawing at him, calling him gutless and screaming that he would beat him by himself. Jones got real hot

116

*and he hit Jackie with the next pitch. Jackie
just got up laughing and jogged to first base.
"I'm gonna steal, I'm gonna steal," he's yelling
at him. Sure enough, he steals second. "I'm
gonna steal third, I'm gonna steal third." Then,
in a flash, he has third stolen. By now you can
fry an egg on old Sam's face, he's so mad. "I'll
steal home, I'll steal home," and he makes one
of those breaks, and Jones bounces the ball in
the dirt. Jackie scores and we win the game by
one run.*[3]

Rickey had known that other teams would try to
intimidate Robinson; in fact, he was counting on it to
rally the rest of the Dodgers to Robinson's side. One
day in Philadelphia, it happened. Led by acid-tongued
manager Ben Chapman, a man who in his playing days
had been run out of New York for making anti-Semitic
remarks, the Phillies were treating Robinson to a barrage of especially nasty insults. Knowing that Robinson
had received anonymous death threats in the mail,
Phillies players pointed bats at him from the bench and
made machine-gun noises. Finally, Brooklyn second
baseman Eddie Stanky decided he had had enough and
challenged the Phillies bench. "Why don't you guys
go to work on somebody who can fight back," Stanky
yelled, "there isn't one of you has the guts of a louse."
Dodgers team leader and shortstop Pee Wee Reese also
stuck up for Robinson; the two soon became fast
friends. Of course, friendship had its limits. In a way
typical of professional athletes, most of the white
Dodgers concentrated on baseball and instinctively
avoided anything that smacked of politics or other
unpleasant facts of life. There were times when his
teammates let Robinson down without ever really
thinking about what they were doing. Brooklyn travel-
ing secretary Harold Parrott told the story of a time

when the Dodgers team bus stopped at a whites-only restaurant in Florida in 1948. Robinson and catcher Roy Campanella had to eat in the bus while their teammates were served in a private dining room. Parrott described the two players' reactions:

> As I juggled the tray of plates onto the lonely bus in the dark, I found a Robinson who was politely grateful—but seething at the put-down. Campanella was pleading to avoid a scene: "Let's not have no trouble, Jackie. This is the onliest thing we can do right now, 'lessen we want to go back to them crummy Negro Leagues."
>
> Robinson's eyes were aflame, and I knew what was racing through his mind. He had played a part in winning fat World Series checks for all those guys inside the restaurant, even the third-string bullpen catcher and the humpties who hardly ever got into a game. And there they were, all of them stuffing the food down and seeming not to care that he wasn't one of them.
>
> He had taken the abuse without a whimper; the dusters and beanballs they threw at him didn't stop him from getting up and socking the big base hits to prove that he really belonged. But what was the good of the "big experiment" when here he was, still on the outside?[4]

Campanella tore into his meal, Parrott remembered, but Robinson did not touch a bite. By the end of his rookie year, things may not have been easy for Robinson, but at least his teammates valued his contributions on the field, and few were openly hostile. Playing under incredible pressure, subject to all kinds of off-the-field distractions, and true to his word to Branch Rickey not to retaliate against racist attacks, Jackie Robinson hit .297 with 31 doubles, 12 home runs, and a league-

*During the Dodgers 1947 spring-training camp,
Jackie Robinson studies the team's player roster.
Robinson had performed well for the minor-league
Montreal Royals in 1946, and he opened the
1947 season as the Dodgers starting first baseman.*

leading 29 stolen bases. When the 1947 season was over, Jackie Robinson took home the NL Rookie of the Year award and an ulcer.

Rickey's plan to destroy the baseball color line had succeeded, and there was no turning back. Bill Veeck, the owner whose attempt to integrate the 1944 Phillies had been narrowly thwarted by Landis, signed outfielder Larry Doby for the Cleveland Indians, and Negro League stars began to cross the color line in a slow but steady stream. Willard Brown, Hank Thompson, and Dan Bankhead came in late 1947. In 1948 they were joined by Roy Campanella and Satchel Paige. Along with Jackie Robinson, players like these brought with them the fast, exciting Negro League style of baseball, reviving dead-ball tactics like the stolen base and hit and run in a major-league game that had become boring and one-dimensional in its overreliance on the home run. In 1950 Branch Rickey was forced out by new Dodgers owner Walter O'Malley. He went to Pittsburgh, where he rebuilt the Pirates farm system, stole the great Roberto Clemente from the Dodgers, and laid the foundation for the team's rebirth in the late 1950s. He was elected to the Hall of Fame in 1967, at least in part for his role in the breaking of the color line.

THE YEAR: 1947

The year of Jackie Robinson began with another controversy: the Durocher affair. The fall guy in a feud between the Dodgers' Branch Rickey and the Yankees' Larry MacPhail—MacPhail had gone to work for the Yankees after his return from the war—Durocher had also got himself in trouble with the commissioner's office for associating with gamblers and unsavory types like actor George Raft and gangster Bugsy Siegel. Smarting from criticism that he was a do-nothing commissioner and resentful of the fact that he was overshadowed by the legend of Kenesaw Mountain Landis, Chandler was also looking for someone to suspend, preferably for a gambling-related offense. Just before the 1947 season, Durocher received a one-year suspension from Happy Chandler for "an accumulation of unpleasant incidents." Burt Shotton took over as Brooklyn's manager for the 1947 season; Durocher's Dodger career came to an end in mid-1948, when he moved to New York as manager of the Giants.

All this momentarily distracted baseball fans from the fact that the Dodgers had purchased the contract of first baseman Jackie Robinson from Montreal. Robinson opened the season as the first black major leaguer since the Walker brothers had played in the American Association in 1884. To add to the obvious pressure on Robinson, in the beginning his teammates were far from friendly. For weeks, none of them sat near him or ate with him; some refused even to speak to him. Things finally began to change when Robinson's aggressive, running brand of baseball helped move Brooklyn into first place. Robinson hit .297, scored a team-high 125 runs and led the NL in stolen bases with 29; he was later voted NL Rookie of the Year. With Robinson, Pee Wee Reese, Dixie Walker, and Pete Reiser all hitting for average—and without a legitimate power threat—the Dodgers led the league in stolen bases and on-base average on their way to a 94–60 record, five games better than St. Louis. Cardinal Harry Walker won the batting title at .363, and New York's Johnny Mize and Pittsburgh's Ralph Kiner shared the league-lead in homers with 51; Boston third baseman Bob Elliot, who hit .317 and drove in 113 runs, was voted NL MVP.

On July 4, Cleveland owner Bill Veeck signed outfielder Larry Doby. Jackie Robinson's success in the NL had taken all the air out of the idea that black players could not deal with the pressure or the competition of major-league ball; it also made a bit of an anticlimax out of the arrival of Doby, the first African-American to play in the American League. A second baseman by trade, Doby—who remains overshadowed by Jackie Robinson and underrated by posterity—came up in late 1947 and was converted to a centerfielder for the 1948 season. There he batted .301 and showed both good power and a good batting eye. To the dismay of anti-integrationists, the Indians won the pennant just as Robinson's Dodgers had done the year before. Now just another winning ballplayer, Doby went on to score or drive in 100 runs in a season eight times. In 1952 he hit 32 homers to become the first black player to lead either league and repeated this feat in Cleveland's 111-win, pennant-winning 1954 campaign. St. Louis became the second AL club to sign African-American players when it inked Hank Thompson and Willard Brown. A reunited Yankees team scored the most runs in the AL, 794, allowed the fewest, 568, and ran away with the flag by 12 games over Detroit. While defending champion Boston stumbled out of the gate due to injuries to starters Tex Hughson, Boo Ferriss, and Mickey Harris, New York tied an AL record with a 19-game winning streak and never looked back. MVP Joe DiMaggio hit .315 with 97 runs, 97 RBIs and 61 extra-base hits, and Tommy Henrich drove in 98 runs on 35 doubles and an AL-high 13 triples. Allie Reynolds went 19–8 and reliever Joe Page made 56 appearances, compiled a 2.46 ERA and recorded 17 saves. Ted Williams produced another great season that had no impact on the pennant race; he won the Triple Crown with a .343 average, 32 home runs, and 114 RBIs. He also led in runs with 125 and drew the most walks ever, 162, by anyone not named Ruth.

Yankees pitcher Spud Chandler retired in 1947 with a 109–43 record and the highest winning percentage in history, .717. Also retiring were Mel Ott, who is now fourteenth all-time in homers with 511, sixth in walks with 1708, and ninth in both runs and RBIs, and Hank Greenberg, who is fifth in career slugging at .605.

New York defeated Brooklyn in a seven-game World Series, as Spec Shea went 2–0 with an ERA of 2.35 and Johnny Lindell drove in seven runs. The highlight of the series was game four, when Bill Bevens took a no-hitter into the ninth inning. With two outs and two on, pinch hitter Harry "Cookie" Lavagetto doubled to win the game for Brooklyn by a score of 3-2.

There is no question about Branch Rickey's central role in the story of the breaking of the baseball color line. What is not so clear, however, is whether Rickey's version of the hows and whys of the story are entirely accurate. As for Rickey's motives, while he himself did not deny that his primary purpose was to sign winning ballplayers, Rickey claimed to oppose segregation on moral grounds. There was the Charley Thomas incident when Rickey was coaching Ohio Wesleyan. As Rickey once said, "I couldn't face my God much longer knowing that His black creatures are held separate from His white creatures in the game that has given me all I own." The problem with this statement is that Rickey was 65 in 1946; he had spent 42 years in professional baseball. At no other time had he made any protest over organized baseball's Jim Crow policies. During the two decades that Rickey ran the St. Louis Cardinals, the Cardinals were the only team in the majors to have racially segregated stands. Even the St. Louis press box was segregated. Years later, Rickey claimed that he had tried behind the scenes to desegregate the stands, but it is hard to understand what would have stopped him if he had. The Cardinals owner, New Yorker Sam Breadon, was one of the more liberal owners about race, and no city or state law required white and African-American fans, or reporters, to be segregated at the St. Louis ballpark. There is no independent evidence that Rickey ever made any effort to desegregate the ballpark or the pressbox.

Fellow baseball owner Bill Veeck and others have also doubted whether Branch Rickey's original and only purpose in scouting Negro League ballplayers was really, as he claimed, to find the right man to break the color line. Is it possible that in the beginning, Rickey was serious about starting a new Negro League called the United States League and that, in the beginning at least, he was scouting Negro League players to sign them for the Brown Dodgers? That might explain why Rickey instructed Sukeforth to hide his presence from the management of the Negro League teams he was scouting. "Mr. Rickey told us," Sukeforth later said, "he didn't want this idea of his getting around, about the Brooklyn Brown Dodgers, that nobody was supposed to know what we were doing." When he scouted Negro League games, Sukeforth was told to sit in the stands like an ordinary fan and not let on why he was there. This makes a lot of sense if Rickey was plotting to rob the Negro Leagues of their players and form a competing league. The reason for such secrecy, however, is not so clear if the Brown Dodgers were just a cover story. The purpose of a cover story is to cover the truth; why keep a cover story a secret? Finally, when Rickey met with Negro League catcher Roy Campanella and pitcher Don Newcombe in October 1945—after he had already signed Robinson—and offered them contracts, both players came away with the impression that Rickey was trying to sign them for the Brown Dodgers, not the Montreal Royals or Brooklyn Dodgers. It is hard to imagine how Newcombe, who actually signed a contract, could have been mistaken about what team he was agreeing to join.

One explanation for all of this would be that Rickey was moving cautiously toward breaking the color line in the early to mid-1940s but that he was not sure when or even if it would be possible. If the experiment of putting Jackie Robinson in Montreal failed, then he had a backup plan. The backup plan was to go ahead with the United States League and the Brown Dodgers. If his new, white-owned Negro League succeeded, Rickey would very likely damage or destroy the existing Negro Leagues, but he would gain control of a vast pool of baseball talent. If integration came to baseball afterward, Rickey would then have his pick of African-American talent for the Dodgers. Rickey certainly felt no sympathy for the Negro Leagues, which he often described as a "racket" run by gangsters. Like any good politician, Branch Rickey was a master at appearing to lead events that were actually leading him. Rickey spent his whole professional life trying to amass as much baseball talent as possible. All that untapped Negro League talent must have tempted Branch Rickey more than anyone else in organized baseball, especially during the war years when good white players were so scarce. It would certainly have been in character for him to have tried to get his hands on that talent any way he could and work out later how best to exploit it.

The most plausible answer to the question of why Branch Rickey broke the baseball color line and signed Jackie Robinson is that that he thought Jackie Robinson could help the Dodgers win—and that in the ambiguous racial climate of 1947 he thought he might be able to get away with signing him. The bottom line is that Rickey was the one who, in the short term, benefited the most from the breaking of the color line. Jackie Robinson was able to play in the major leagues, although at great personal cost. African-Americans in general gained a few major-league jobs but lost the Negro Leagues, one of the country's largest African-American-owned businesses; the Negro Leagues went broke almost immediately after 1947. As soon as African-American fans realized that integration had come to stay, they flocked to major- and minor-league parks to see their favorites play on white teams. The hundreds of ex–Negro Leaguers who did not get jobs with white clubs were left unemployed. Branch Rickey and the Brooklyn Dodgers, however, got Jackie Robinson, Dan Bankhead, Roy Campanella, Don Newcombe, Sandy Amoros, Joe Black, and Junior Gilliam—the talent base for a Dodgers dynasty that won seven pennants and one World Series between 1947 and 1956. For all of this talent, they paid exactly nothing.

CHAPTER NINE

"*I* Never Had It Made": The Life of Jackie Robinson

The real hero of the breaking of the baseball color line was not Branch Rickey but Jackie Robinson. The grandson of a slave, Jack Roosevelt Robinson was born in Georgia in 1919, the year of the infamous postwar race riots in Chicago and other cities. The family moved to Southern California when he was young. A college sports star at UCLA, he was that school's first four-letter man.

During World War II Robinson served in the army as a lieutenant and morale officer for an African-American unit stationed at Fort Hood, Texas. Fort Hood was a difficult situation, because African-American soldiers may have been fighting and dying alongside white soldiers in Europe and in the Pacific, but back home in the states they were still segregated and discriminated against within the military. Racial tensions, especially at bases in the Deep South, were high. Robinson refused to play baseball at Fort Hood, for example, because the teams were segregated. By insisting on equal access for African-American soldiers to facilities such as the PX, Robinson had already been labeled a troublemaker.

Then came an incident that ended Robinson's army career for good. Sitting in the middle of an army bus at Fort Hood, Robinson was ordered by a white bus driver to move to one of the rear seats, "where," the driver said, "colored people belong." Robinson refused and then got into an argument with a white captain who had been summoned by the driver. The captain had Robinson court-martialed for insubordination. He was acquitted, but the trial embarrassed the army and Robinson was soon honorably discharged, ostensibly because of a bad ankle suffered playing football in his college days.

It is a sad statement about the state of race relations in America in those days that the best job that the clean-cut, college-educated Robinson could find was playing baseball with the Kansas City Monarchs in the Negro Leagues. The Monarchs played him out of position at shortstop—Robinson did not have a shortstop's arm—but he could run and hit and he established himself as a promising young player. In his sports columns, African-American journalist Wendell Smith picked him as the young player most likely to be chosen first to cross the baseball color line. Besides the 1945 tryout with the Red Sox, Robinson worked out for White Sox manager Jimmy Dykes in 1946.

When he entered organized baseball with the IL Montreal Royals, Jackie Robinson dazzled white fans with his aggressive, run-oriented Negro League style of play. "His bunts, his steals and his fake bunts and fake steals humiliated a legion of visiting players," wrote sportswriter Roger Kahn. Displaying what Rickey called his "sense of adventure," Robinson stole home with a frequency not seen in the major leagues since the 1910s and made Houdini-like escapes from run-downs. His daring was all the more impressive because of the unimaginable pressure and loneliness of his early years with the Royals and Dodgers. In 1949, his finest season,

Jackie Robinson slides into third base during the 1952 World Series. In his ten major-league seasons, Robinson excited Dodgers fans and foes with his aggressiveness on the base paths.

he scored 122 runs, drove in 124 and led the league in stolen bases with 37 and in batting at .342.

THE YEAR: 1948

Baseball came within one game of having an all-Boston World Series in 1948, as the Braves went 91–62 to take the NL flag by 6½ games over St. Louis, and the Red Sox finished the regular season tied with Cleveland at 96–58.

Except for 20-game winner and ERA-leader Harry Brecheen, the Cardinals pitching was well below pennant-caliber, as St. Louis trailed Boston in team ERA, 3.91 to 3.38. But 27-year-old second-time MVP Stan Musial made up for his team's thin pitching all by himself; Musial had the finest all-around season of his career, leading the NL in batting at .376, runs with 135 and RBIs with 131. He also led the league in hits with 230, doubles with 46, triples with 18, on-base average at .450, and slugging at .702. Musial came within one home run of leading the NL in every major offensive category, as Johnny Mize and Ralph Kiner tied for the league-lead in homers with 40 to Musial's 39. The Cardinals outfielder's 429 total bases were 113 more than runner-up Mize and the sixth-largest total in history after seasons by such immortals as Babe Ruth, Rogers Hornsby, Lou Gehrig, Chuck Klein, and Jimmie Foxx. The Boston Braves were sparked by Bob Elliot, who hit 23 homers and drew 131 walks, and .300-hitters Eddie Stanky, Al Dark, Tommy Holmes, Mike McCormick, and Jeff Heath. On the pitching side, the Boston fans' cry was "Spahn and Sain and two days of rain." Thirty-year-old righty Johnny Sain went 24–15 to lead the NL in wins, complete games with 28, and innings with 315, and he was third in ERA at 2.60; 27-year-old lefty Warren Spahn went 15–12 with 16 complete games and 257 innings. No other Braves pitcher won over 13 games. Boston led the NL in team ERA, complete games, and fewest walks allowed.

The AL race was still up for grabs at the All-Star break among Cleveland, Philadelphia, New York, and Boston. Joe DiMaggio led the AL in home runs with 39 and RBIs with 155; Tommy Henrich led in runs with 138 and triples with 14. But as the second half wore on, the best hitting team, Boston, and the best pitching team, Cleveland, pulled away from the pack. The Red

Sox featured batting champion Ted Williams, whose home run total slipped to 25, third on his own team behind Bobby Doerr's 27 and Vern Stephens's 29; Dom DiMaggio, who hit 40 doubles and scored 127 runs; and Johnny Pesky, who was tied with Williams for third in the AL in runs with 124. Williams batted .369, but lost out in the MVP voting to Cleveland shortstop and batting title runner-up Lou Boudreau, who hit .355. Cleveland also had second baseman Joe Gordon, who hit 32 home runs; Ken Keltner, who put together a career year with 31 homers and 119 RBIs; and outfielder Dale Mitchell, who batted .336. But the Indians' main strength was their deep pitching staff, with two 20-game winners in Gene Bearden and Bob Lemon, a 19-game winner in Bob Feller, and spot starters Steve Gromek, Sam Zoldak, and Satchel Paige, who went a combined 24–10. Bearden and Lemon led the league in ERA at 2.43 and 2.82, and Feller and Lemon led in strikeouts with 164 and 147. Cleveland owner Bill Veeck was widely ridiculed for pitching ancient ex–Negro League star Satchell Paige—his exact age was unknown, but he was definitely pitching for the Birmingham Black Barons in 1928—but Paige quieted his critics by going 6–1 with a 2.47 ERA. He went on to pitch four more years in the big leagues, going 28–31 with 32 saves and a 3.29 ERA over 179 appearances, mostly in relief.

A coin flip determined that the one-game AL pennant playoff would be played at Fenway Park in Boston, and almost 30 years to the day before Bucky Dent's famous 1978 home run over the Green Monster, shortstop Boudreau won the pennant for the Indians with two home runs over Fenway Park's left-field wall. Cleveland then proceeded to make it a clean sweep of Boston, defeating the Braves four games to two. Feller had a bad World Series, going 0–2 with a 5.02 ERA, but

Cleveland beat the Braves in six games on great pitching performances by Bearden, Gromek, and two-game winner Bob Lemon.

Nineteen forty-nine was also the year that Branch Rickey, sure that integration was here to stay in baseball, released Robinson from his promise to turn the other cheek. After that, the NL felt the fire of the real Jackie Robinson. In 1947 and 1948 he had endured all sorts of racist heckling from the Phillies and their manager Ben Chapman without answering back; Robinson even agreed to pose for a photograph shaking Chapman's hand. When Chapman started in on Robinson again in 1949, however, Robinson answered, "You son of a bitch, if you open your mouth one more time I'm gonna kick the shit out of you." Having sold the public an image of a saintly Robinson willingly turning the other cheek, the press was not happy with the change. As Robinson put it in his 1972 book *I Never Had It Made*:

> I learned that as long as I appeared to ignore insult and injury, I was a martyred hero to a lot of people who seemed to have sympathy for the underdog. But the minute I began to answer, to argue, to protest—the minute I began to sound off—I became a swellhead, a wise guy, an "uppity" nigger. When a white player did it, he had spirit. When a black player did it, he was "ungrateful," an upstart, a sorehead. It was hard to believe the prejudice I saw emerging among people who had seemed friendly toward me before I began to speak my mind. I became, in their minds and in their columns, a "pop-off," a "troublemaker," a "rabble-rouser." It was apparent I was a fine guy until "success went his head," until I began to "change."[1]

Reporter Dick Young complained that when he was with Campanella or some of the other African-Americans on the Dodgers he could forget about race but that Robinson never let him forget the color of his skin. Hearing this, Robinson laughed and said, "did it occur to you that I don't *want* Dick Young to forget?"

Jackie Robinson always remained close to Branch Rickey. Disappointed when Rickey left the Dodgers, Robinson retired in 1956 when Dodgers owner Walter O'Malley tried to trade him to the New York Giants. After being elected to the Hall of Fame in 1962 Robinson continued to lead a public life, campaigning with Martin Luther King and speaking out on civil rights. He was never forgotten by the African-American players who followed him across the color line. Don Newcombe said: "Through baseball, Jackie did more to tear down segregation in hotels and sports arenas than any other man. Nobody will ever do more, because it won't be necessary again." Willie Mays was more succinct. "Every time I look at my pocketbook," Mays said, "I see Jackie Robinson." Larry Doby said: "Jackie Robinson went through a lot. We all went through a lot. It wasn't easy being a black man in America in 1947." At the 1972 World Series Robinson criticized baseball for taking so long to finish the job of integration. "Someday," he said, "I'd like to be able to look over at third base and see a black man managing the ball club." Nine days later he was dead of a heart attack at 53. Old friend Pee Wee Reese felt that part of the reason for Robinson's early death was the strain of having been the first to cross the baseball color line. Another factor may have been his frustration at the slow pace at which baseball has changed since 1947. It took almost 30 years for a major-league club to hire its first African-American manager and even longer to hire its first African-American general manager and league president; there still has never been an African-American owner in major-league baseball. "I don't think Jack ever stopped carrying the burden," Reese said. "I'm no doctor but I'm sure it cut his life short."

The courage, determination, and skill of Jackie Robinson was an inspiration to the baseball world and to all of America. Robinson's success in Brooklyn enabled the Cleveland Indians to integrate the AL. In the years after that dozens of all-white minor leagues began to integrate or, in the case of some of the older leagues, to reintegrate. The national governing body of amateur baseball announced that it would allow interracial tournaments and leagues. Formerly all-white professional football signed four African-American players in 1946. Other sports broke their color lines. It is a testament to how much the integration of baseball overshadowed that of the other sports, that few fans today could tell you the names of the first African-Americans in football, basketball, golf, or tennis. Jackie Robinson's impact is still felt, even outside the world of sports, and his name is almost as well known today as it was in 1947.

Source Notes

CHAPTER ONE
1. Joe Durso, *DiMaggio: The Last American Knight* (Boston: Little, Brown, 1995), p. 126.
2. John Tullius, *I'd Rather Be a Yankee* (New York: Macmillan, 1980), p. 148.

CHAPTER TWO
1. Robert Creamer, *Baseball in '41* (New York: Viking, 1991), pp. 65–66.

CHAPTER THREE
1. Michael Seidel, *Ted Williams: A Baseball Life* (Chicago: Contemporary Books, 1991), p. 116.
2. Donald Honig, *Baseball America* (New York: Macmillan, 1985), p. 247.
3. Lee Allen, *100 Years of Baseball* (New York: Bartholomew House, 1950), p. 275.

CHAPTER FIVE
1. Bill Veeck, *Veeck as in Wreck* (New York: Putnam, 1985), p. 185.

2. Ted Williams, *My Turn at Bat* (New York: Simon and Schuster, 1969), pp. 156–57.
3. Peter Golenbock, *Bums* (New York: Putnam, 1984), p. 79.

CHAPTER SIX
1. Lee Lowenfish and Tony Lupien, *The Imperfect Diamond* (New York: Stein and Day, 1980), p. 141.

CHAPTER EIGHT
1. Golenbock, p. 157.
2. Leo Durocher, *Nice Guys Finish Last* (New York: Simon and Schuster, 1975), p. 167.
3. Maury Allen, *Jackie Robinson, A Life Remembered* (New York: Franklin Watts, 1987), p. 116.
4. Golenbock, pp. 196–97.

CHAPTER NINE
1. Jackie Robinson, *I Never Had It Made* (New York: Putnam, 1972), p. 92.

ibliography

Allen, Lee. *The American League Story.* New York: Hill and Wang, 1962.

———. *The National League Story.* New York: Hill and Wang, 1961.

———. *100 Years of Baseball.* New York: Bartholomew House, 1950.

Anderson, Dave. *Pennant Races.* New York: Doubleday, 1994.

Barber, Red. *When All Hell Broke Loose.* Garden City: Da Capo, 1982.

Creamer, Robert. *Baseball in '41.* New York: Viking, 1991.

Durocher, Leo. *Nice Guys Finish Last.* New York: Simon and Schuster, 1975.

Goldstein, Richard. *Superstars and Screwballs.* New York, Dutton, 1991.

Golenbock, Peter. *Bums.* New York: Putnam, 1984.

Greenberg, Hank. *The Story of My Life.* New York: Times Books, 1989.

James, Bill. *The Bill James Historical Baseball Abstract.* New York: Villard Books, 1988.

Johnson, Dick and Glenn Stout. *DiMaggio, An Illustrated Life.* New York: Walker and Co., 1995.

Lieb, Fred. *The Story of the World Series.* New York: Putnam, 1965.

Lowenfish, Lee and Tony Lupien. *The Imperfect Diamond.* New York: Stein and Day, 1980.

Polner, Murray. *Branch Rickey.* New York: Atheneum, 1982.

Reichler, Joseph, ed. *The Baseball Encyclopedia.* New York: Macmillan, 1988.

Robinson, Jackie. *I Never Had It Made.* New York: Putnam, 1972.

Seidel, Michael. *Ted Williams: A Baseball Life.* Chicago: Contemporary Books, 1991.

Spink, J. G. Taylor. *Judge Landis and 25 Years of Baseball.* New York: Crowell, 1947.

Thorn, John and Pete Palmer, eds. *Total Baseball.* 3d ed. New York: HarperCollins, 1993.

Tygiel, Jules. *Baseball's Great Experiment.* New York: Oxford University Press, 1983.

Veeck, Bill. *Veeck as in Wreck.* New York: Putnam, 1962.

Williams, Ted. *My Turn at Bat.* New York: Simon and Schuster, 1969.

Index

140

About the Author

Thomas Gilbert has published many books and articles on baseball history, as well as a biography of Roberto Clemente. For Franklin Watts, he has written Baseball and the Color Line and the previous titles in this series—Elysian Fields, Superstars and Monopoly Wars, Dead Ball, The Soaring Twenties, and The Good Old Days. Mr. Gilbert lives in Brooklyn, N.Y.